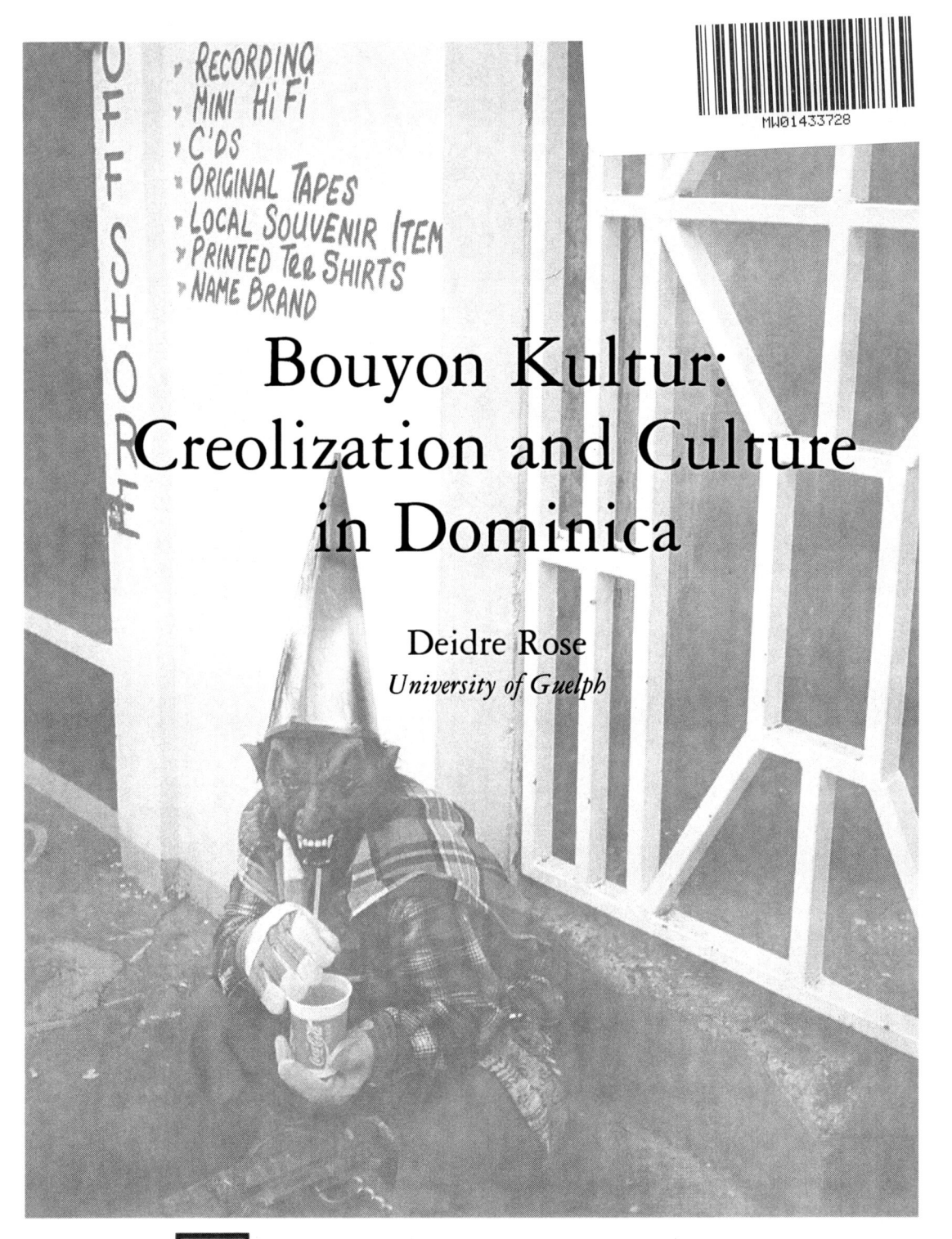

Bouyon Kultur: Creolization and Culture in Dominica

Deidre Rose
University of Guelph

KENDALL/HUNT PUBLISHING COMPANY
4050 Westmark Drive Dubuque, Iowa 52002

Cover image provided courtesy of the author.

Copyright © 2009 by Kendall/Hunt Publishing Company

ISBN: 978-0-7575-6037-8

All rights reserved. No part of this publication may be reproduced, stored in a retrieval system, or transmitted, in any form or by any means, electronic, mechanical, photocopying, recording, or otherwise, without the prior written permission of the copyright owner.

Printed in the United States of America
10 9 8 7 6 5 4 3 2 1

PART 1

ETHNOGRAPHIC SETTING

1
INTRODUCTION: RE(DIS)COVERING THE CARIBBEAN

ABOUT THIS STUDY	3
ON THE CARIBBEAN AS ETHNOGRAPHIC REGION	3
CHALLENGES TO THE CONCEPT OF CULTURE: HYBRIDIZATION, SYNCRETISM, AND CREOLIZATION	4

2
"APRES BONDIE C'EST LA TER" – DOING FIELDWORK IN DOMINICA

MY ARRIVAL	16
CLIMATE AND GEOGRAPHY	19
ECONOMY	20
PEOPLE	25
RESEARCH METHODS	27

PART 2

CREOLE FESTIVALS AND FOLKLORE IN DOMINICA

3

PLANTATION SOCIETY AND THE MIRACLE OF CREOLIZATION

PRODUCTION AND LABOR ON THE PLANTATION	33
GENDER RELATIONS ON THE PLANTATION	37
THE GENESIS OF CREOLE CULTURES IN DOMINICA	41

4

HERITAGE DAY, CELEBRATING CREOLE CULTURAL EXPRESSIONS

CREOLE CULTURE	46
A BRIEF HISTORY OF HERITAGE DAY AND INDEPENDENCE DAY	47
THE START OF THE SEASON – JING-PING	48
DRESS: WOB DWIYET, JUP, AND NATIONAL DRESS	49
JOUNEN KWÉYÒL – CREOLE (LANGUAGE) DAY	50
HERITAGE DAY 1996: SCOTTS HEAD SOUFRIERE	50
CONCLUSION	55

5

CARNIVAL MONARCH COMPETITIONS AS A "THIRD SPACE"

A BRIEF HISTORY OF CARNIVAL	59
CARNIVAL IN DOMINICA—1997	61
CONCLUSION	65

6

FOLKLORE, GREETINGS, AND MORALITY IN DOMINICA

THE MOUS, A PARABLE	71
GREETING PROTOCOLS, "BEVERLY HILLS" AND "NASTY GIRLS"	73

PART 3

GLOBALIZATION: CONTACT AND CULTURAL CHANGE

7

CONTINUITY AND CHANGE: **CREOLIZATION AND GLOBALIZATION TODAY**

CHANGES IN DOMINICA'S ECONOMY	88
TOURISM	90
FUTURE RESEARCH DIRECTIONS	96

LIST OF **REFERENCES**   101

ACKNOWLEDGEMENTS

My life in Dominica was enriched by the many people who went out of their way to facilitate my research and provide me with guidance. I would like to first express my gratitude to all those people, especially Marcia Dublin and the other members of Dominica's Movement for Cultural Awareness, members of the Cultural Division, and the workers at Front Line Books. Marcel Fontaine and Gregory Rabess were also very helpful. Friends and neighbours in Dominica, too numerous to mention by name also taught me a great deal. Thomas, Monika, Cheryl, Marissa, Tarissa, Shadina, Samantha, Ashma, Adaina, Chrissie and their families all deserve special mention.

Two years of my field work in Dominica were funded by the University of Toronto, Open Fellowships. Professors and mentors, in particular my academic advisor Michael Lambek and committee member Richard Lee, guided me through the dissertation process. Teresa Lewitsky of the Data Resource Centre at the University of Guelph helped create the map. My husband and fellow academic Gregory Cameron provided useful comments on earlier drafts of this manuscript. Published works by Dominican scholars, including Lennox Honychurch and Daryl Philip were very helpful, as was the linguistic material compiled by Marcel Fontaine.

Student interest in and enthusiasm for the stories told on these pages alerted me to the need for an accessible, written version to complement lectures. I would also like to extend my thanks to Angela Puls and Alexis Sciuk at Kendall/Hunt Publishers, for their support and encouragement.

Most importantly, I would like to extend my warmest thanks and appreciation to the people of Dominica who shared so much of their lives and their stories with me during the periods of fieldwork. I dedicate this book to the people of Dominica at home and overseas, with respect and admiration. *Tjenbé wed*!

A NOTE ON PRONUNCIATION OF ANTILLEAN KWÉYÒL

Kwéyòl is one of the languages spoken by the majority of the people in Dominica, and several words in this text are written in Kwéyòl. Itself a product of creolization, the Kwéyòl language combines African grammar structure with a French-derived lexicon. A detailed discussion is found in Chapter 4. Readers might find the following guide to pronunciation helpful.

CONSONANTS

Most consonants correspond with their English and French counterparts; however, there are two exceptions:

Ch — "sh" as in "she"

Tj — "tch" as in "watch"

VOWELS

As in the French language, vowels may be written with an accent. These may be unfamiliar to the English reader.

An — "aw" as in "awe"

É is pronounced "ay" as in "bay"

É is pronounced "eh" as in "get"

En is pronounced "ahn" as in "on"

I is pronounced "ee" as in "ski"

PART 1
ETHNOGRAPHIC SETTING

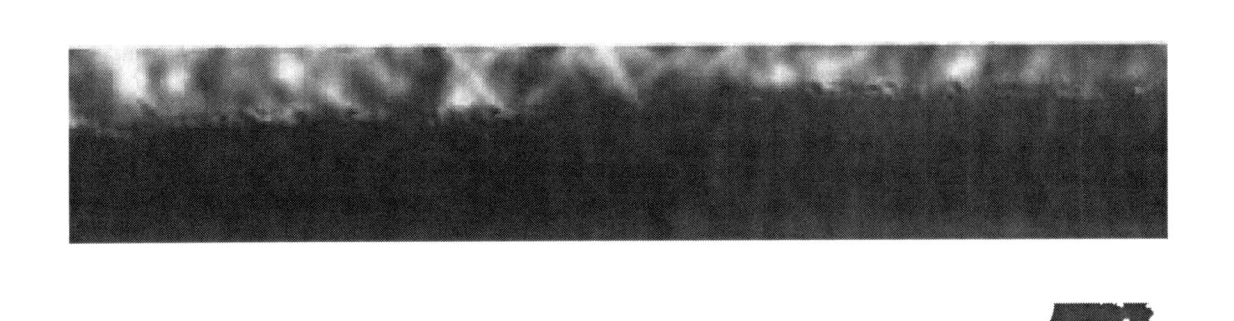

ABOUT THIS STUDY

This book is based on fieldwork conducted in the Commonwealth of Dominica, an island nation located in the Eastern Caribbean. Dominica is one of the larger islands found in the chain referred to as the Lesser Antilles (see map, page 15 of chapter 2). I first went to Dominica in August 1996, and returned four times spanning through May 2001. Since my last visit, I have continued to follow the changes taking place on the island through participation in on-line forums, reading newspaper and academic accounts, and staying in touch with Dominican friends in Canada and in Dominica.

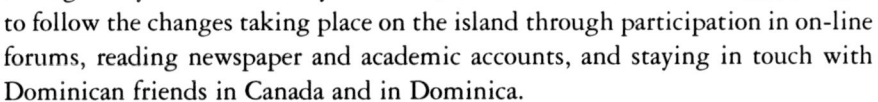

My initial interest in Dominica focused on the relationship between performances, identity, and social change. The research originally emphasized popular theatre for social change and I worked closely with two popular theatre troupes operating on the island: The Movement for Cultural Awareness and The People's Action Theater. Both of these groups were involved in events that entertained and edified participants using theatre as a medium for communication. Plays and workshops dealing with social issues such as environmentalism, self-esteem for youth, and AIDS awareness and prevention were included in the repertoire of these groups. Events that emphasized tradition, heritage, and national identity also fell under their province. It was also these latter events that sparked a new interest for me as a fieldworker, for throughout my many extended visits, people constantly shared stories ("folklore"), and brought me to national and village level events that explicitly celebrated a uniquely Dominican, Creole identity through dance and music. These celebrations of cultural heritage and Creole identity, metaphorically referred to as *bouyon* by many Dominicans, are the subject of this book. Before turning to the ethnography, some words on the theoretical discussion of which this text is but one contribution are in order.

ON THE CARIBBEAN AS ETHNOGRAPHIC REGION

At the turn of the twentieth century, the relatively new discipline of anthropology had begun its project of ethnographic analysis based on fieldwork. Important changes had been made in terms of theoretical questions and methodological approaches. The most significant of these was the method of participant observation, based on prolonged fieldwork and involvement in the community under study. However, there remained a preference for small-scale, relatively isolated and pristine groups. For this reason, ethnographic study of the peoples of the Caribbean was limited, as anthropologist Michel-Rolph Trouillot has put it, the Caribbean is "nothing but contact." Here there are few "natives," and cultural forms found in the region are primarily the result of this sustained state of contact—in short, creole cultures. If this characteristic of the region made it too fuzzy for earlier anthropologists, it is this same characteristic that has led to renewed interest in the region on the part of scholars from a wide range of social sciences, including anthropologists (Munasinghe 2006). The contemporary analyses of the types of social change brought on by the processes of globalization have provided the impetus for this renewed interest.

Over the past two decades, the Caribbean region has been rediscovered by social scientists in various disciplines who are seeking to understand contemporary conditions of globalization and postmodernity. With the (re)turn to the Caribbean region, "creolization" has come to serve as the root metaphor describing contemporary conditions of postmodernity: transnationalism, pastiche, blurred boundaries, and mobility. In this era, the argument goes, people, commodities, and ideas are moving across the globe at unprecedented levels (Hannertz 1992; Stewart 2007). The effects of all this movement include the growth of corporations conducting business in more than one country (transnationalism); increased blending to create new cultural forms (pastiche); and a breakdown of national and group boundaries. This book seeks to explore the processes and products of creolization through an ethnographic study of the Commonwealth of Dominica, an island which has previously received little scholarly attention (exceptions are Baker 1992; Trouillot 1988; and Quinlan 2004).

CHALLENGES TO THE CONCEPT OF CULTURE: HYBRIDIZATION, SYNCRETISM, AND CREOLIZATION

Cultural borrowing and interpenetration are today seen as part of the very nature of cultures. To phrase it more accurately, syncretism describes the process by which cultures constitute themselves at any given point in time. Today's hybridization will simply give way to tomorrow's hybridization, the form of which will be dictated by historico-political events and contingencies.
Stewart 1999:41

WHAT IS CULTURE?

At the origin of the discipline of anthropology, Edward Tylor defined culture, "Culture . . . is that complex whole which includes knowledge, belief, arts, morals, law, custom and any other capabilities and habits acquired by man as a member of society" (Tylor 1871/1958: 1, quoted in Kottak 2007: 41). Since Tylor the concept of culture has been highly contested. Today there are several ways of defining culture and it will be worth clarifying how the term will be used in this text before turning to the ethnographic material that forms the bulk of this study. Culture is an abstract set of values, beliefs, and perceptions of the world that when acted upon produce behaviors considered appropriate by members of the society that shares the same culture. Characteristics of culture include that it is learned, shared, dynamic, and integrated (Kottak 2007: 41–44). Let us look at the implications of these characteristics. First, culture is learned. It is not connected to a person's biological make-up, it is acquired through learning from parents, teachers, friends and neighbours. Second, culture is shared. It is something that a person acquires and acts upon as a member of a group. Third, culture is dynamic. Culture is not a fixed or static thing, it is a set of attitudes and ways of seeing the world that may be modified through changes in environment, technology, changes in knowledge, contact with members of other groups with different sets of attitudes, etc. Finally, culture is integrated. Parts of the system will support other parts; so, for example, changes in technology may effect changes to other parts of the cultural system. These aspects of culture are important to understand because culture is not a thing, it is relational and abstract.

"Creole" is a term applied to the cultures of the Caribbean region by both anthropologists and members of the societies in the Caribbean region to indicate a distinctive feature of the cultures of these societies. Creole cultures emerge through processes of creolization, processes that bring/brought about changes in attitudes and practices through sustained interaction of peoples from various cultures.

WHAT IS CREOLIZATION?

The concept of creolization emerged in the sixteenth century and came to have different uses and meanings in different contexts and at different times (see Box 1.1 for a summary of the uses of the word creole, used to apply to the results of creolization). The term was originally used in Spanish colonies, where their term *"criollo"* is reported to have been created using a combination of the two Spanish words *criar* (to create, to imagine, to settle) and *colon* (a colonist, a founder, or a settler) (Brathwaite1974: 10). Initially the term had a pejorative connotation

> **BOX 1.1**
>
> # USES OF THE WORD CREOLE
>
> Criollo (creole): Early colonial period, Spanish colonies. Used to denote people of European descent born in the colonies.
>
> Creole: Mid-colonial period. Used to denote people of "mixed descent".
>
> Creole: Linguistics. Used to denote languages that combined European lexicon and West African grammar structures
>
> Creole: Especially in French colonies. Used to denote all cultural forms that exhibited elements of mixing different traditions to create something new. Applied to dress, music, language, cuisine, and dance.
>
> Source: Adapted from Stewart 2007.

and was used to differentiate the offspring of European settlers born in the colonies from people born in Europe. The assumption was that these individuals, by virtue of the tropical climate or proximity to non-European populations, were somehow inferior to European-born individuals. By contrast, in Dominica, as in much of the British Caribbean, the term *creole* is used to designate something local which is the result of a blending of various ingredients that originated elsewhere. Dominicans use the cooking term *bouyon*, metaphorically, to describe their own particular version of creole. Bouyon, which comes from the French word bouillon, is a type of cooking that involves the blending of a number of flavours into a type of stew. In the dish, each item retains its distinct shape but is infused with the flavours of all of the other ingredients. An apt metaphor, as we shall see.

This ethnography will analyze three sites of cultural production, Carnival, Heritage Day, and a series of everyday narratives or parables ("folktales") I label "morality tales" which highlight the especially Dominican idea of creole or bouyon. Heritage Day and Carnival are two events within a series of performances marking two of Dominica's major "cultural seasons." These are two events in which Dominicans present images of themselves to themselves and these festivals represent two concrete moments of the self-conscious reflection and negotiation indicated in theories of cultural hybridity or creolization. While in Dominica, I was accommodated in every possible way to ensure my attendance at these events, in which people seemed to take great pride. Heritage Day represents a commemoration of the past traditions representative of the colonial era and Carnival represents a celebration of both the historical moment of Emancipation and contemporary negotiations of the processes of hybridization resulting from globalization today. By contrast, the folktales discussed in Chapter 6 focus on everyday notions of moral comportment and moral personhood. The idea of "consciousness" provides the emic thread in local discussions of who is and is not entitled to membership in the moral community. A person achieves moral personhood through the performative enunciation of a normative moral character rooted in the value orientation of reputation and respectability.

This ethnography draws on the Dominican concept of *bouyon*. As mentioned earlier, bouyon is a cooking term used metaphorically to describe a style of music (of the same name), culture, and society in Dominica. The idea of "bouyon" is explored through events such as the Carnival Queen Competition of 1997, a major event in the days preceding Carnival. Here, the "negotiation of difference" in what Bhabha (1994) has termed a "third space" is evidenced through the various talent entries and costume designs. One skit, "The Dominica Story" is particularly revealing in that it refers specifically to "bouyon" as a metaphor for Dominican society. The performances, particularly the Carnival Queen competitions, indicate that notions of "moral integrity" and the performative enunciation of a normative moral character, or more simply, questions about what it means to be a proper citizen, are at the heart of these negotiations.

HYBRIDITY AND HYBRIDIZATION

Theories about hybridity have undergone numerous shifts as the concept has moved from biology to social science. Today it is used in linguistics, semiotics, and post-colonial cultural theory. A brief review of the history of the concept of hybridity reveals a set of ideas about purity/impurity and the perils of moral degeneration entailed in diluting pure categories, especially as related to colonial encounters. The concepts of hybridity and hybrids were developed in the practice of botany and then biology in the nineteenth century. A hybrid was an animal or plant produced from the mixture of two species. Hybridity implies the creation of a new species as a result of the combination of two discrete species. It was originally believed that the human "races" were in fact separate species, hence the term *mulatto*—a mule being the sterile offspring of a horse and donkey. Colonial encounters soon proved this theory false; however, the proponents of "scientific racism" were not easily dissuaded. Victorian era scholars revised their theories in rather creative ways to produce theories which clearly sought to uphold notions of superiority of one "race" over the others.

The concept has more recently been developed in cultural and literary theory where it has been used to intervene in binary constructions of difference (male/female, white/black, colonizer/colonized). For example, Homi Bhabha argues that cultural identities are not based upon pre-given, cultural scripts. "Coloniser" and "colonised" are not separate, independent entities. Rather, the negotiation of cultural identity involves the continual exchange of cultural performances. The performances occupy a liminal space, a hybrid site for the production and reflection of cultural meaning:

> *Terms of cultural engagement, whether antagonistic or affiliative, are produced performatively. The representation of difference must not be hastily read as the reflection of pre-given ethnic or cultural traits set in the fixed tablet of tradition. The social articulation of difference, from the minority perspective, is a complex, on-going negotiation that seeks to authorize cultural hybridities that emerge in moments of historical transformation.*
>
> *Bhabha, 1994: 2*

For various reasons, including the racialist connotations of the term "hybridity," many scholars prefer to use the term creolization. However, as we have seen, creolization may also have negative connotations. In either case, to privilege the derogatory meanings is to repeat the violence of privileging the views of the dominant classes at the expense of the views of the people who consider themselves creole. The purpose of this ethnography is to demonstrate the ways that concepts that resemble hybridity or creolization are used, and indeed celebrated—on the ground—by the many peoples whose history is intimately, and at times violently, tied to the various notions of "mixing" carried by both terms.

Throughout both Latin America and the Caribbean, local concepts and practices have emerged that celebrate creolization. Indeed, creolization has served a role in various independence movements and in (re)claiming national cultures (Anderson 1991). As the creolité movement in the French Caribbean demonstrates, the concept is alive and well:

> *At the heart of our Creoleness we will maintain the modulation of new rules, of illicit blending. For we know that culture is never a finished product, but rather the constant dynamic search for original questions, new possibilities, more interested in relating than dominating, in exchanging rather than looting.*
>
> *Bernabe, Chamoiseau, Confiant & Kyher 1990: page 54*

As Mimi Sheller (2003: 196) suggests, by "returning to the Caribbean roots of the concept of creolization," and "regrounding it in its specific social and cultural itineraries, we might recover the political meanings and subaltern agency that have been barred entry by the free-floating gate-keepers of 'global' culture." This ethnography aims to make a contribution to this project of situating creolization in its original context through an examination of the celebration of hybridity, creolization, and various creole cultural forms in Dominica.

BOUYON KULTUR: A LOCAL CONCEPTION OF HYBRIDITY

During the period I was in Dominica, the term "bouyon" was used in a variety of contexts to refer to Dominican society and culture:

> *If you look up the word "boullion" [sic] you will get the idea. The only difference is that you must bear in mind the nutritive value of the bouillon, it having absorbed all the best of the various foods it has drawn from. The liquid from a one-pot consommé, that is the bouyon. The best of the lot!*
>
> Anji

> *Bouyon to me is a mélange; a mixture or everything mixing in one like a soup or broth.*
>
> Anonymous

And finally,

> *If you want to know what bouyon means, go to (Delphis site "definitions").*[i]
>
> Anonymous

The style of music created by the innovative WCK (Windward Caribbean Kulture) Band was the first, to my knowledge, to apply the concept of bouyon explicitly to refer to their innovative style of music. WCK is a popular Dominican group, and their bouyon music incorporates the sounds of the traditional Jing-Ping bands with modern "hi-fi" music and uses synthesizers, electric guitars, and a *lapo-kabwit* (goat-skin drum). WCK's press sheet describes the band:

> *The four man strong performing group based in the capital of the island, Roseau, has definitely earned its place at the top of the ranks of dance music entertainment due to its unique blend of the island's traditional music and dance—namely Belle, Quadrill [sic], Jing Ping, Masouk, and Kadance.*
>
> *The end result? A music which they call Bouyon (Boo-Your). CK, for short, has managed to bring the traditional sounds of Dominica through the use of up-to-date musical instruments thus enhancing and revitalising this once dormant sound.*[ii]

In Dominica, as stated above, there are two cultural seasons in particular that provide examples of the kind of performances where the processes of hybridization past and present, are performed, Heritage Day (Chapter 4) and Carnival (Chapter 5). Jing-Ping bands provide the musical accompaniment for a number of European-derived dances including the Quadrille, Heel and Toe, step dances, and waltzes. These dance styles and the accompanying sounds are a prominent feature of Heritage Day and Independence Day ceremonies and a series of cultural shows and competitions beginning early in September and carrying on until Independence Day (November 3). It is also the music for sèwènol, a Christmas season practice in the Carib Territory.[iii] This traditional style of music has insinuated itself in Carnival celebrations thanks to the popularity of hi-fi bands, especially WCK. However, Jing-Ping is the dominant musical form heard during Independence and Heritage Day celebrations.

THE ORGANIZATION OF THE TEXT

The body of this ethnography is organized into three parts. Part I provides a description of the research setting and methods, as well as a brief synopsis of Dominica's history. Part II focuses on the celebration of various creole cultural forms enjoyed by members of the Dominican community. Specifically, this section focuses on ethnographic descriptions of some of the major cultural performances associated with Heritage Day, Carnival, and "folklore." The performances associated with Heritage Day explicitly celebrate cultural forms created during the Plantation Era: Creole language, dress, cuisine, and music. The performances associated with Carnival provide a celebration of freedom and, as we shall see, exhibit signs that the processes of creolization are continuing today. Next, we will look at Dominican folklore, stories passed on that reflect and reinforce certain ideas about moral or proper social behaviour. The Carnival Queen Competition in particular provides an illustration of the Dominican concept of *bouyon*, which resonates with academic literature on cultural hybridity. It is the concept of bouyon that provides the emic thread for these chapters. Chapter 6 further examines the idea of "consciousness" through an analysis of parables ("folklore") and beliefs that define criteria for membership in Dominica's moral community. These also provide models for marginalization and exclusion. Part III returns to an exploration of questions about globalization, contact, and cultural change in Dominica today. Here we will look at the effects of tourism, migration, and mass-produced music forms on the continuing evolution of Dominican cultural forms.

The organization of the material into discrete parts reflects three stages in my fieldwork. During the first phase, many of the Dominican people I met went to great lengths to provide me with an education in what I now understand to be Dominica's moral system. This is detailed in Part II and forms the bulk of the ethnographic analysis.

It is now my belief that the lessons learned through attending (and sometimes participating in) the cultural performances during Heritage Day and Carnival, and listening to narratives ("folklore") were what the people of Dominica most wanted to teach me. The observations recorded here were made at events where people celebrated their history and their cultural traditions. Part III, by contrast, describes events that transpired during my fieldwork, but it also includes events that occurred and information that I collected after my second prolonged stay. But there is another reason for my decision to present the material in this order, and for my understanding of why the material was shown to me in the order that it was. This stems from a telephone conversation with my good friend Marcia, a key interlocutor throughout my research period. Some time after my return to Toronto, I mentioned to Marcia that I had the feeling that some of my instructors and friends suspected me of "going native." She asked what that meant, and I loosely explained that it meant I had become Dominican. Her response surprised me. "Of course you did, Dee. We made you so."

CHAPTER **SUMMARY**

Key Terms

BOUYON - Dominican Kwéyòl for a type of cooking. Also used as a metaphor to refer to Dominican society and culture.

CREOLIZATION - A theory that describes and analyzes the processes and results of social change brought about by the prolonged interaction of peoples from more than one cultural or ethnic group.

EMIC - The anthropological term for the insider's perspective or viewpoint.

HYBRIDITY - A term taken from botany, used metaphorically to refer to the results of social or physical changes brought about by the mixing of genres or types.

GLOBALIZATION - A term used to describe the processes of interconnectedness—social, political economic and cultural—that are extending to all or most parts of the world today.

POSTMODERNITY - A term used to describe a state of flux, movement, crossing of national borders, and rapid social change said to characterize much of the world today.

SYNCRETIC - Typically used to describe the reconciliation of more than one religious belief system to create a new religion. Sometimes used to describe the products of creolization more generally.

Discussion Questions

1. What are some of the ideas about culture outlined in this chapter?

2. What is the significance of the distinction between the emic and etic views?

3. Compare the Dominican concept of "bouyon" with the Canadian metaphor of the "mosaic" or the American metaphor of the "melting pot."

4. What are some of the key debates about the terms "creolization," "hybridity," and "syncretic"?

5. According to the author, what is the link between the condition of postmodernity and the renewed scholarly interest in the Caribbean region?

6. Think about a Canadian or American tradition that displays elements of hybridity.

WEB - LINKS

RACE: Are We So Different? A Project of the American Anthropological Association.

http://www.understandingrace.org/home.html

FURTHER **READING**

Anderson, Benedict 1991.

Imagined Communities - Reflections on the Origin and Spread of Nationalism. London and New York: Verso.

Stewart, Charles (ed.) 2007.

Creolization: History, Ethnography, Theory. Walnut Creek, CA: Left Coast Press Inc.

NOTES

[i] Delphis is the name of a web-site featuring information about Dominica.

[ii] The sound is not, in fact, dormant and to my knowledge it never has been. This comment reflects, I think, a division between town and country and a tendency for certain "traditional" cultural forms to be muted except around Independence Day celebrations in the capital but which thrive in other parts of Dominica. Another example of this is the museumification of certain artifacts which are displayed as part of the past on event days, but of which onlookers can be heard to comment, "But I still use that, wi." For example, irons which are heated by coal and the "coal pot."

[iii] I had the good fortune to accompany a troupe during one night of Sèwènol in December 1998. The musicians met in a bar at 10:00 pm to "warm-up." At midnight, we all piled into a pick-up truck and a van and headed out. At our first stop I got the idea. The band members gathered on the porch or under a window and the leader began to call out in Creole, teasing the sleeping residents about what they might be doing. The band then broke into loud music until the residents woke up and let us in. The band was then supplicated with rum (or, traditionally, money) and continued to play a few songs and visit. When the band members were satisfied with their "payment," we moved on to the next house. This continued until 8 o'clock in the morning, and I was very glad I was given the option of coffee or juice by all of our hosts!

2

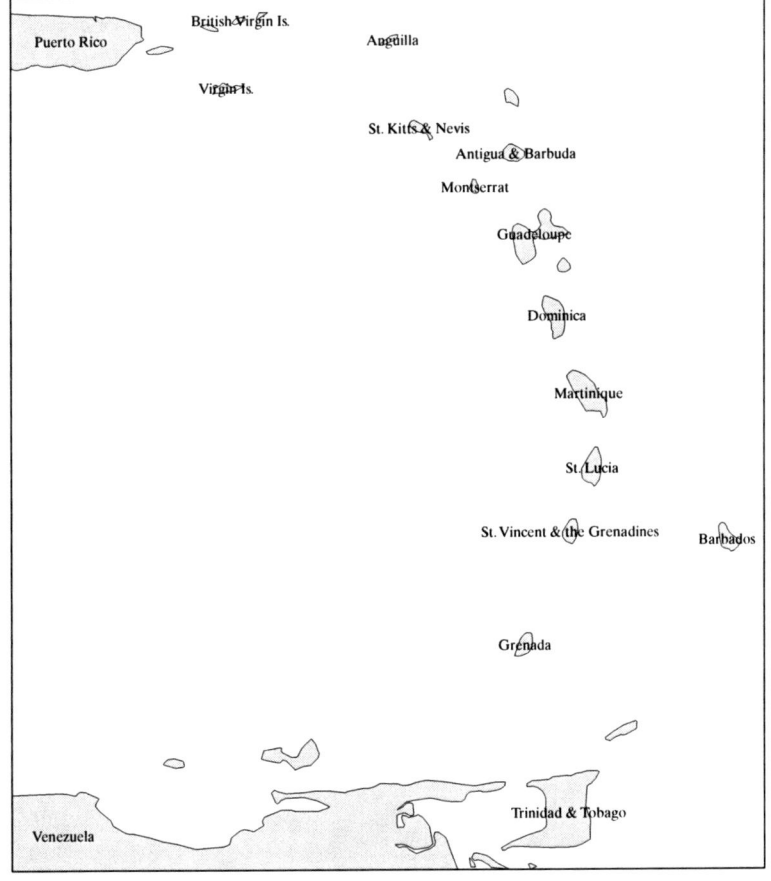

"APRES BONDIE C'EST LA TER" – DOING FIELDWORK IN DOMINICA

MAP 1

Windward and Leeward Islands.

Dominica's official motto, and the title of this chapter, translates as: "After the good Lord [we love] the soil." This motto reflects both the religiosity of the majority of the population and the country's longstanding dependence upon the agricultural sector for economic survival.

Dominica is located in the Eastern Caribbean. It is the largest of the Lesser Antilles, an archipelago located in the Eastern Caribbean Sea. A rainforested, mountainous tropical island of 298 square miles with a population of approximately 70 000 people, Dominica has some narrow coastal plains, but most of the arable land is on steep slopes. Slaveholding colonizers established sugar, coffee, and tobacco plantations on the few flat areas (See Box 2.1). For the most part even the slaveholding estates were relatively small in size. Indeed, during colonial times, the terrain and weather combined to give Dominica the nickname "The Whiteman's Graveyard"—referring to the likelihood a planter would become bankrupt. The Kalinago (a.k.a. the Carib), who occupied the island when Christopher Columbus first spotted it on November 3, 1493, call the island *Waítukubuli,* which means "tall is her body." The island is so mountainous that it is rumoured that Christopher Columbus, when describing the island to Queen Isabela, crumpled up a piece of paper and threw it on a table. The mountainous interior is largely inaccessible due to the lack of roads and an abundant growth of lush tropical rainforest.

Historically, this topography has provided a natural fortress and was a factor enabling Carib resistance to would-be Spanish settlers who made repeated attempts at colonising the island during the 16th and 17th centuries. Indeed, all that remains of Spain's early interactions with Dominica's first inhabitants are the island's name and a legend of a buried treasure, booty taken from Spanish ships that had fallen victim to storms or attacks during that period (Rose, 2009). By the 1690s both French and British settlers began to call Dominica their home. France and Britain both made claims to Dominica, which was officially ceded to Britain at the Treaty of Paris in 1763. Although Dominica has been an independent nation since 1978, its colonial history is reflected in Dominica's languages, culture, and political economy. Dominica's official language is English, but the majority of the population also speaks Kwéyòl, a French-based Creole. Cultural festivals, like Carnival, revolve around the calendar of the Roman Catholic Church and blend West African and European cultural elements (See Box 2.2 for a list of annual festivals). The school system is based on the British model; the electric company, the telephone company, and several banks are British owned, and the economy is dependent upon the export of a limited number of export staple crops to the United Kingdom.

MY ARRIVAL

To get to Dominica by air, one first has to travel to another island as there is no international airport. After reading Patrick Baker's (1994) description of his precarious landing at Dominica's Melville Hall Airport, I decided to spend the night in Antigua and take a flight to Canefield Airport the next morning. I arrived in Dominica on a Sunday. To board the plane, the other passenger and I had to balance on a couple of rope steps. We could not talk during the flight as the noise of the engine(s?) was too loud. The flight was bumpy, noisy, and quick—we arrived at Canefield about 45 minutes after departing. The plane bounced off the tarmac and the runway was too short for the plane to come to a full stop—we were heading straight for the Caribbean Sea when the pilot, with great skill, turned the plane around 180 degrees as the plane continued to bounce along the tarmac and finally came to a full stop. I deplaned and went to face the immigration and customs personnel. The customs agent looked at my bags and said, "That all for you?" I felt like the most selfish person on the planet as I replied, sheepishly, "Yes." He waved me through with a cursory, "Okay, then." The next stop was immigration. Before leaving Toronto, I had checked with the Dominican consulates in Ottawa and New York, and had a travel agent check for me. All three checks resulted in the same answer: Persons from a Commonwealth country do not require a visa to stay in Dominica for a period of 12 months or less. Unfortunately, nobody had passed this information along to the immigration department in Dominica. I discovered that I did indeed need a visa, and, as it was Sunday, this business would have to wait for a visit to town the next day.

Once I was out of the airport I found a taxi to take me to the hotel I had booked for the first few days. The driver, a middle-aged Rastafarian man, made a few inquiries about who I was, where I was from, and what brought me to Dominica and I asked a few questions about the view from the window. We passed a small industrial park, a few small villages, through Roseau, then through two areas I later learned are known as the "Gaza Strip" and "Montego Bay." Dominicans, one friend later told me, "have a name for everything." I passed through these areas, known for their "roughness" many times in the months to follow and got to know many of the "ghetto boys" who patrol the streets and often harass passers-by—especially foreign women. Through time, these same young men became my friends and protectors and their teasing became gentler.

"TOWN"

Dominica's capital is Roseau. The buildings are low, none higher than four stories, and are made of old stone and wood. The roads are cobbled in places, paved in others, and full of potholes. A few goats and chickens share the sidewalks and roads with pedestrians. On the sides of the roads hucksters—sitting with cardboard boxes or baskets full of fruit, home-made candy, store-bought gum (2-pack Chiclets), crab-backs (a tasty cooked crab salad served in the shell, with the claw serving as a spoon), bakes (fried dumplings, called "Johnny Cakes" in the north part of the island), fresh juice, or clothing and shoes—ply their wares. Some of these vendors, almost all women, have rather elaborate booths that they assemble when they arrive in the morning, then take apart for the journey home.

Chapter 2   "Apres Bondie C'est la Ter" – Doing Fieldwork in Dominica

For many people who live in the rural areas (the majority of the population), "town" is a place to be avoided if possible. For most of Dominica's Rastafarian population, "town" is "Babylon" and "country" is "Zion." For others who make the trek from their village to their jobs in the hospital, government buildings, stores, or offices, town is simply where they work. Many of the people who live in Roseau have other property in the countryside, where they retreat as soon as the workweek is over. A walk through town on any Sunday will leave you feeling as if you are in a ghost town, there are so few people about and so few businesses open—a stark contrast to the busy, if slow-paced, weekdays in town.

Dominicans refer to Roseau and Portsmouth (the major town in the north) as "town." Both towns are home to schools, department and grocery stores, doctors, lawyers, dentists, a marketplace, and roadside stalls. Roseau is the home of the government buildings. Both towns also have a police station and a courthouse. Buses (mini-vans) with names like "Pepsi" and "Skettle" arrive, filled with passengers, at their designated spots where they wait until they are full again before making the return trip to their home village. People stop and greet friends, neighbours, and relatives that they meet by chance on the city streets and vehicles stop in the road as they pass each other to say hello or perhaps pass on a message for someone whom the driver will encounter on his route. Faced with the urgent task of getting a visa, I got to know town and many of the bus drivers and residents quite well early on.

New to the country, I had to ask for directions to the government building, police headquarters, doctor's offices, and the hospital. Concerned people would give me the directions, and even walk part of the way with me to make sure I was able to see my destination, and of course, to find out why I needed to see that particular sort of official. At the police station I was photographed, fingerprinted, and interviewed; a process I understand is the same when one is under arrest. Immigration also required an extensive medical examination. The form that the Immigration Officer at the government building gave me included boxes for "Insanity," "Venereal Diseases," and "Alcoholism" along with a host of other pleasant-sounding ailments and character flaws. I asked around for a doctor, specifying that I would like to see a female doctor and found that there were two women with private practices in Roseau. The doctor laughed at the outdated form, and filled in the forms that I would need to get the required tests at the hospital. I found the hospital and was given a blood test and a chest X-ray (testing for HIV and tuberculosis). It took four months to get my Visa—the medical tests, interviews, and police reports told the officials that I was not carrying an infectious disease, was not apparently insane, and had no known criminal record. But the final say was, I later learned, in the hands of my neighbours who, in police interviews, said that I was "a nice lady" because I always said hello. At the time, I had no idea how significant greeting protocols are in Dominica's code of moral comportment. Across the country there was a general notion that respect accompanies certain comportment. However, it seemed that not everyone agreed on what that comportment was. For example, some people believed that respect accompanies certain occupations—for the majority these occupations are teacher, nurse, and mother. Lawyers, doctors, judges, politicians, and other members of the elite were not necessarily owed respect (in the minds of the majority of the population). For the vast majority, however, adherence to greeting protocols, dress, and appearance were significant factors in the relative degree of respect one was entitled to. Respect, was in many ways, a matter of reciprocity. These matters are the subject of Chapter 6.

I settled myself in a village in the southwest of the country, relatively close to town, on a well-treed mountainside for the first twelve months of my stay. When I returned in October 1997, another tenant occupied that house, so I took a smaller house along the main road on the northwestern coast. This house was removed from any village and had no running water, but boasted a stunning view of the mountains on either side and behind, and a view of the Caribbean Sea about 1000 feet below.

CLIMATE AND GEOGRAPHY

BOX 2.1

DOMINICA'S CLIMATE AND GEOGRAPHY

Geographic Coordinates:	15° 25° N, 61° 20° W
Area:	754 sq km
Coastline:	148 km
Climate:	tropical; heavy rainfall
Terrain:	rugged mountains of volcanic origin
Natural Resources:	timber, hydropower, arable land
Natural Hazards:	flash floods; hurricanes

Source: Adapted from the CIA World Factbook Dominica, https://cia.gov/library/publications/the-world-factbook/print/do.html

Dominica's interior comprises mainly tropical and semi-tropical rainforest. Dominica has two seasons, as many Dominicans told me, "rainy and wet." The average rainfall is 250 inches a year in the interior and 70 inches a year on the coast. Dominica is rumoured to have 365 rivers; one for every day of the year, however, some of the rivers are now dry and the Layou River, Dominica's longest and largest, was destroyed in a massive landslide in the fall of 1997. (The river has since been dredged and is flowing once again). The wettest months, June to October, dovetail with hurricane season. A popular Dominican rhyme provides a mnemonic for the season:

> *June too soon,*
> *July stand by,*
> *August you must,*
> *September remember,*
> *October all over.*

During the period of my fieldwork, Hurricane David, which had devastated the country in 1979, was still on people's minds. People are still able to point out damage David left in its wake, and refer to the time immediately after with a nostalgic "people really pulled together then."

With only two climatic seasons, "rainy and wet," people mark the passing year with references to cultural events that dominate each month. For example, Independence Day (November 3) and the six weeks prior to Independence Day are filled with festivals and other cultural events celebrating the cultural creativity of the Plantation Era. Carnival season, which celebrates Emancipation, extends from December 26 to midnight on Shrove Tuesday.

The steep slopes that mark most of the island's interior and the susceptibility to hurricanes are the ecological factors that combine with historical factors to explain Dominica's long-standing economic dependence on the export of bananas to the United Kingdom.

ECONOMY

Dominica is the poorest country in the English-speaking Caribbean—and was even before events in the world economy stifled their principle industry—banana export. Most Dominicans I know become angry when they hear reports of their country's poverty and many people told me, "We may not have money, but we have food." Twiggy, a young man who was about to attend college, asked me why in Europe, where people had so much money, did people allow some to die of rickets and scurvy just for want of fruit? In Dominica, he assured me, such a thing could never happen. Despite its relative poverty, people in Dominica boast high life expectancy, and enjoy healthy diets thanks to the abundance of fish, rainfall, and fertile land. Prior to 1995, when the new government (responding to structural adjustment demands) introduced user fees at the hospitals, most people also had access to adequate health care services. Dominicans also share an ethos of caring, so that when a person (especially a child) requires health care that exceeds the capacity of Dominican facilities, community members collect money and a few wealthy families contribute the balance to meet the required fees to send the patient overseas for treatment.

At the time of my fieldwork 67 percent of the labour force was employed by the banana industry, primarily as peasant farmers, packers, truck drivers, or employees of the Dominican Banana Marketing Association. This number has been greatly reduced over the past decade. (See Box 2.2 for a summary of Dominica's economy.) Many Dominicans engaged in multiple occupations. Some bus drivers doubled as tour guides when a cruise ship was in port and many men worked informally in this capacity as well. The tourist sector was a growing source of employment, employing tour guides, taxi drivers, hotel workers, bartenders, servers, cleaners, receptionists, and souvenir vendors. The government and service sectors were also major sources of employment. Women dominated in the marketplace and comprised the majority of the hucksters. Women also sold sweets and snacks from streetside stalls or from a window at their homes, took in laundry, and ran the majority of the rum shops and snackettes on the island. There was also a small sector of professionals including lawyers, doctors, engineers, and one psychologist.

However, as stated above, the major economic sector was agriculture. The present economy has its historical roots in the slave-based plantation system of the French and British colonial regimes that controlled the country at one time or another in its history. During the Plantation Era (period of slavery) estates practiced monocrop agriculture (growing one crop) for export to Europe and America. Slaves were given some basic provisions which included salt, salt cod or smoked herring, basic clothing or fabric, and a ration of flour. They lived in chattel houses that they built themselves, and were given a small plot of less-desirable land on which they were required, in addition to their labours in the fields, to grow the bulk of their own food. Any surplus produced remained the property of the slave who could sell it at the marketplace. Some people were able to purchase their freedom this way; others used the monies earned for food, entertainment or fabric to make dressy clothes.

Following Emancipation on August 1, 1838 newly freed slaves left the estates and established squatter settlements. Many freed men and women cultivated their own small plots, selling any surplus in the local markets. A marketing system was already in place as a result of the Sunday sales of surplus crops described above (cf. Honychurch 1995). Archival sources highlight the reluctance of newly freed slaves to engage in contract labour for former slave-owners. Indeed, much of Dominica's economic history in the period immediately

BOX **2.2**

DOMINICA'S ECONOMY

GDP Composition by Sector:

    Agriculture   17.7 %
    Industry   32.8%
    Services   49.5%

Labor Force:

    25000 (2000 est.)

Labor Force by Occupation:

    Agriculture   40%
    Industry   32%
    Services   28%

Unemployment Rate:

    23% (2000 est.)

Population Living Below Poverty Line:

    30% (2002 est.)

Agricultural Products:

    Bananas, Citrus, Mangoes, Root Crops, Coconuts, Cocoa

Industries

    Soap, Coconut Oil, Tourism, Copra, Furniture, Cement Blocks, Shoes after Emancipation describes the numerous strategies employed by the colonial government and the planter class to try to force the new peasant class into wage labour for the estates. Troulliot (1988) has argued that the development of a peasantry in Dominica was a form of resistance that enabled people to maintain a level of independence by limiting their engagement with the cash economy. Former slaves continued to produce for subsistence, selling the surplus in the local market. The colonial government, mainly through the imposition of taxation, forced many people into wage labour on estates producing crops for export to the United Kingdom. Despite significant historical changes—the shift from slavery to independent production or wage labour, for example—the majority of the population remained in agricultural production, and Dominica has continued to export tropical fruits through both inter-island and international trade. Farmers also produce a surplus to sell in the Saturday markets in Roseau and Portsmouth, and to local hotels. Early in the last century, bananas became the prominent export crop. The importance of the banana industry to Dominica's culture and economy was a frequent topic of conversation with people I met. Some discussion of this industry, therefore, is necessary for a full understanding of the cultural material that is the focus of this monograph.

WHY BANANAS?

Prior to 1930, the banana was not an export commodity but was used as a "shade tree" and consumed locally. The principal export crops were cocoa and limes, crops needing protection from the sun when young. There was, however, a small scale inter-island trade in bananas shipped from Portsmouth, the major city and port on the northwest side of the island (Mourillon, nd: 9). However, Dominica was hit by hurricanes in 1928 and 1930 which destroyed the lime orchards, effectively putting an end to the lime industry as lime trees take up to eight years to resuscitate. In 1931 Mr. A.C. Shillingford found a market overseas and began to ship the "Gros Michel" banana to Liverpool on Leyland Line steamships. "Then in 1933 representatives of the Canadian Banana Company, a subsidiary of the United Fruit Company, expressed their interest in the banana trade; however, they were not prepared to deal with individual growers. Legislation was enacted in March 1934 establishing the Dominica Banana Association to market bananas and to regulate and control banana export" (Mourillon n.d.: 9). A five-year contract with the Canadian Banana Company was signed in March 1934 and the first shipment left Dominica on April 16 of the same year. By the end of 1934 the biweekly shipments had increased from approximately 1,000 bunches to 2,500 bunches. (A "count" bunch had nine full hands and weighed about 40 pounds.) (Mourillon n.d.: 10–12). So by 1934 the banana trade was growing steadily.

The industry faced many challenges, however. For one thing, Dominica lacked sufficient roads, making it difficult for small-holders in remote areas to get their produce to port. Another problem was that the Gros Michel variety of banana is susceptible to Panama disease. By 1937 the Canadian Banana Company was accepting only high-grade bananas free of scars. World War II brought problems in shipping, which stopped altogether in 1942 after the Canadian National Steamship boats were destroyed by enemy action. The British government stepped in with a War-Time British Subsidy to "relieve small-holders, who had been depending exclusively on bananas for a livelihood" (Mourillon n.d.: 13). These trends: the demand for high-quality, unblemished bananas and the granting of subsidies to ensure Dominican small-holders continued to produce bananas remained in place until the World Trade Organization (WTO) ruling in 2000.

One of the factors that led to the adoption of the banana crop as a staple export was that there was an existing market in Europe and North America. From a geopolitical and economic standpoint a number of factors combined to create this market. Beginning in the 19th century, new technologies in mass transportation (steamship and rail) combined with the availability of cheap land and labour in the tropics to make the banana a viable economic investment. The rise of multinational corporations and the processes of industrialization and the development of mass markets in Europe and North America led to the entities that would exploit and consume, respectively, this new commodity (Nurse and Sandiford 1995: 1). Another factor was the decline in the sugar industry (Nurse and Sandiford 1995: 26). The presence of an existing market, and the decline in another major export crop were significant factors in Dominica's turn to banana export, but there were other factors as well.

From an ecological standpoint, the banana is a viable plant because it is a perennial, it grows well on the steep slopes, its canopy provides shade for other plants that are grown between the rows of banana trees, the refuse from the tree provides mulch, and it has a relatively high yield per acre (Nurse and Sandiford 1995: 16). Another important benefit of the banana tree is that it has a short gestation period (nine months). Thus, growers can quickly rehabilitate it after hurricane damage (Nurse and Sandiford 1995: 78). The crop is therefore well suited to Dominica's ecological niche. Finally, since the majority of Dominica's banana producers are small-holders they produce for their own subsistence as well as for the market. "Fig," or green bananas, have been and continue to be a staple in most Dominicans' diets and are served in some households as a side dish with all meals. Nurse and Sandiford point to the peasant farmers' subsistence ethic of "safety first" and "risk aversion." As we have seen, an established market for bananas was already in place. As a perennial, the banana crop gave farmers a regular biweekly income (Nurse and Sandiford 1995: 79). The importance of the banana crop to Dominica's economy and identity, and people's responses to the threat to their livelihood is the subject of Chapter 7.

PEOPLE

Because my fieldwork involved travelling around the country with the two popular theatre troupes, and because I was invited to so many other special events, I got to spend time in many parts of Dominica and met people across the island. Dominica is an island in which managed presentations of self are of central importance; but, unlike other islands, the dark-skinned majority does not particularly value "whiteness." Indeed, to call someone a "white woman" or *famn blanc* is, in many contexts, an insult.

Except in sections of this ethnography where I explicitly state otherwise, I use the term Dominicans to refer to the majority of people I met and spoke with; people who participated in the workshops, took public transportation, washed their clothes in the rivers—rural and urban poor— and also to the cultural workers—the team members of Dominica's Movement for Cultural Awareness, the people who organized Heritage Day 1996, and members of the Komité Pou Etid Kwéyòl—to name a few. The names of the members of these organizations are their real names, all other names are pseudonyms. I travelled to many villages and spent time in both major towns as well. While I found regional diversity (differently shaped dumplings, different names for certain food items, etc.) the core values that I have teased out of the various performances analysed in this ethnography were evident in the behaviour of people all across the island. There were, of course, a few people who did not share this moral framework, who did not believe in the entities described in Chapter 6 and who thought many of their fellow countrymen "backwards." For example, two men who had spent a significant amount of time living overseas and had earned professional designations implored me not to write about these "backward" country people. However, their attitude was not representative.

During the struggle for Independence, the Black Power and Civil Rights Movements in the United States influenced Dominican activists. However, people involved in the struggle for independence included "Black," "Mixed," "White," and "Carib" Dominicans. To emphasize inclusivity, the group called itself the Movement for a New Dominica, avoiding references to race or colour.

RELIGION

Most Dominicans are deeply religious. Even political meetings begin with prayers or at least a mention of God. Although Dominicans do not restrict their spirituality to institutional settings, churches dominate the landscape and are usually the largest and most grandiose buildings in the country. The majority of the churches, and the majority of the population, is Roman Catholic. There are also a number of people who call themselves "Christians"—the term for all Protestant denominations—and see themselves as distinct from the Roman Catholic majority. There is also a large Rastafarian population, although this

BOX 2.3

PEOPLE

Population: 72514

Age Structure:

   0–14 years   24.7%
   15–64 years   65.1%
   65 and over   10.2%

Life Expectancy at Birth:

   Total population   75.33 years
   Female   78.41 years
   Male   72.39 years

Ethnic Groups:

   "Black"   86.8%
   "Mixed"   8.9%
   Carib Amerindian   2.9%
   "White"   0.8%
   Other   0.7%

Religions:

Roman Catholic 61.4%; Seventh Day Adventist 6%; Pentecostal 5.6%; Baptist 4.1%; Other Christian 13.9%; Rastafarian 1.3%; Other or None 7.7% (source, 2001 Census)

Languages

English (official); French Patois

Source: Adapted from the CIA World Factbook, Dominica.

religion is seldom recognized in any official national statistics. Finally, there is a small Muslim population. B'nai B'rith also has a few adherents on the island.

Rastafarians are often targets of abuse and scorn, but there are also many Dominicans who admire their values. There is a distinction made between true Rastafarians (of which there are more than one type) and "fashion dreads." Fashion dreads are men who sport dreadlocks but do not live their lives according to the tenets of Rastafarianism. Rather, they fancy themselves rebels, and possibly are interested in attracting a white girlfriend. True Rastafarians follow dietary restrictions, most are vegetarians but none will eat pork. As much as possible, Rastafarians will avoid contact with "Babylon" (town) living as far away from "the system" as they can.

Christians (Baptist, Presbyterian, Seventh Day Adventist, and Episcopalian denominations) consider themselves to be more respectable than other Dominicans. Unlike Catholic Dominicans, Christians avoid participation in cultural events like Carnival—they consider events that include dancing, "jumping-up," or costumes to be the work of Satan. One afternoon, I was showing some friends the photographs I had taken during the Carnival parades when a Christian woman entered the shop. She glanced at my photos, mumbled something with a frightened look, made hand gestures in my direction and ran out of the store. I must have looked rather confused, because my friends began to laugh uncontrollably. "What's going on?" I asked. It seems that the woman, on seeing my photos, decided that I was in league with the devil himself and had cast a spell to keep my evil away from her. I asked my friends if she wasn't a bit *fou* ("crazy" or "soft in the head") and they replied "No, she's just a Christian." Christians also avoid alcohol and will exclude a woman from church membership if she gives birth outside of wedlock.

RESEARCH METHODS

The major cultural performances described in the following chapters were observed, and where possible, videotaped. I also attended organisational meetings and/or rehearsals for some of the major events. Sometimes I moved back and forth from audience to backstage, but most of the time I watched the performances from the centre of the audience—seeing what they saw and recording the reactions of audience members nearest to me (or sometimes just the loudest). The stories recorded in Chapter 6 were recorded both in one-on-one interviews and group settings. My access to these performances and stories stemmed from participant observation—living in a village, meeting people in town and villages, and making friends with some of the cultural workers involved in the planning and production of these events.

Much of my understanding emerged or developed during the conversations and interactions with the people I was surrounded by; in this sense part of the study was "naturalistic" (Sobo 1993: 27). Most of the background information was collected while washing clothes in the river, buying supplies in a local shop, watching a daily soap opera with others in a village shop, crammed together with other passengers in crowded buses, or while watching dominoes games. I interviewed community health workers, actors and theatre organisers, Kwéyòl advocates, and people on the street. I spoke with people of all ages, and of varying degrees of closeness—from virtual strangers to people who have become life-long friends. I occasionally spoke with people from the elite classes, but more often not.

Because this ethnography focuses on the processes of creolization in Dominica, the next chapter will explore historical shifts in the island's economic base and the social structures that dominated each respective phase of Dominica's interaction with the global economy—plantation society, the proto-peasantry, and contemporary times.

CHAPTER SUMMARY

Key Terms

NATURALISTIC STUDY - One based primarily on impressions gathered through daily participation in the lives of the people being described.

PARTICIPANT OBSERVATION - One of many fieldwork methods that emphasizes, as the name suggests, participating to the extent possible, in the daily lives of the people about whom the anthropologist intends to write.

Discussion Questions

1. What were the fieldwork methods employed by the author?

2. Why was the banana crop important to Dominica's economy?

3. Why does the author place quotation marks around some of the ethnic groups listed in Box 2.3?

4. What are Dominica's major industries?

5. What are some of the key ecological and geographical features of this island? What are the benefits and challenges posed by this environment?

WEB - **LINKS**

A Virtual Dominica

http://www.avirtualdominica.com/home.cfm

The World Factbook, Dominica. CIA

https://www.cia.gov/library/publications/the-world-factbook/geos/do.html

FURTHER **READING**

Myers, Gordon 2004.

Banana Wars: The Price of Free Trade (A Caribbean Perspective). London and New York: Zed Books.

Van Maanen, John 1988.

Tales of the Field: On Writing Ethnography. Chicago and London: The University of Chicago Press.

VIDEO

Singer, Andre (director) 1985. *Bronislaw Malinowski: Off the Verandah*.

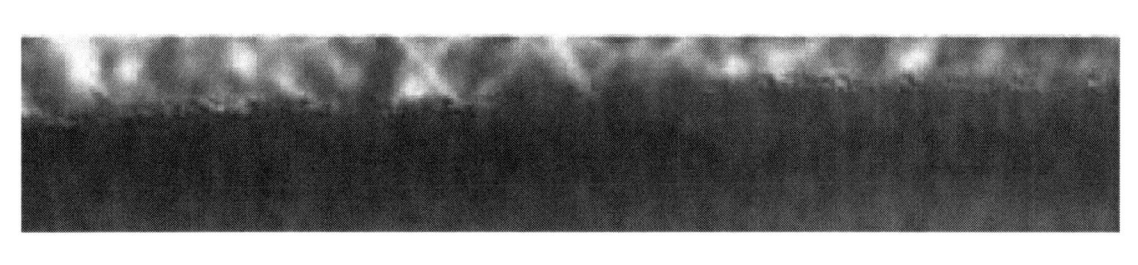

PART 2
CREOLE FESTIVALS AND FOLKLORE IN DOMINICA

From the family plots of the Jamaican hinterland, the Afro-religions of Brazil and Cuba, or the jazz music of Louisiana to the vitality of Haitian painting and music and the historical awareness of Suriname's Maroons, the cultural practices that typify various African American populations appear to us as the product of a repeated miracle. For those of us who keep in mind the conditions of emergence and growth of ideals, patterns, and practices associated with African slaves and their descendants in the Americas, their very existence is a continuing puzzle. For they were born against all odds.

Trouillot 2002: 191

As mentioned in the previous chapter, Dominica was colonized by both the British and French. It was during the height of the Plantation Era, the period of history marked by the harsh conditions of slave labour on coffee, cotton, and sugar plantations that the processes of creolization began. In this chapter we will look more closely at the conditions under which Dominica's creole language, dress, music, and dance were created.

PRODUCTION AND LABOR ON THE PLANTATION

Although European settlers inhabited Dominica since at least the seventeenth century, it was not until after 1725 that slavery on a large scale came to the island, making it one of the last islands in the region to experience plantation agriculture and social relations. French planters introduced coffee to the island and, for a period, these estates brought the planters much wealth. Records for 1765 show that Dominican plantations exported 20 100 pounds of cacao; 969 900 pounds of coffee; and 226 095 pounds of cotton that year (Goodridge 1972: 154). The sugar plantations, introduced to the island by the British, were potentially profitable as well, although the climate and terrain did make sugar production a bit precarious. Work on all plantations was arduous. In the case of coffee, slaves had to cut and burn the forested areas of land and prepare the fields for the planting of coffee. Steep slopes were made viable by a system of terracing, cutting, and leveling the land to prevent soil erosion. The fields, once planted, also had to be continuously weeded to protect the coffee trees. Ground provisions were planted between the trees, benefiting from the shade and some of these provisions, such as cassava, also provided some cash income for the planters (Honychurch 1995: 72–3).

By the end of August, the trees were mature and ready for harvest. Slaves worked from early morning until late afternoon, with only a short break at midday. Before the mid-day break and at the end of the work day, the slaves' baskets would be checked to ensure that they had harvested a sufficient volume of coffee berries. Those who had not met their quota would be punished by up to six lashes of the whip (Honychurch 1995: 73).

After harvesting, the berries were processed. First they were put through a mill to remove excess skin. Next the berries were washed and then spread out on a drying platform. On the French plantations, this platform was called the *glacis*. Once dried, the beans were stored in a granary and then sorted by old or sick slaves and children, who were charged with separating the good-quality beans. Each estate then operated more or less as its own factory, growing and processing its own product. The labour force and buildings were organised along the most efficient and economical lines possible. The finished product was also packed on the estate before being shipped off to the coffee shops of Europe.

The sugar estates were organized along similar lines. Sugar estates required special buildings such as boiling and curing houses, a distillery, workshops and a sugar mill. Some plantations also had an infirmary for the sick and a small prison house to hold slaves. As with the coffee plantations, these plantations operated like factories and the sugar was grown, harvested, and processed on the estate. With the infirmary and prison facility, these plantations were like small scale societies of their own.

PLANTATION SOCIETY

The plantation society was rigidly hierarchical, with set groups established along lines of production and social status. Most of the British plantations in Dominica were run by managers or attorneys while the owner remained in Britain or lived on another island in the Caribbean. French planters, by contrast, were more likely to live on their plantations, and this had effects on the creole culture that was to emerge, as we shall see. The population on a plantation consisted of various Europeans (usually French or British), West African peoples, and sometimes indentured labourers, poor Europeans who had borrowed money for passage or who had been sentenced to labour for committing some petty crime. Typically, Europeans were the minority in terms of population size but, with the exception of indentured labourers, usually held the most economic and political power (See Box 3.1 for some 18th century population statistics). The manager or planter was at the top of the hierarchy and had the most control over his own labour and that of others working on the plantation. Most of the planter and manager class were men.

Next on the scale of command was the overseer who kept track of financial accounts and made sure that the slave driver and field workers were working at a sufficiently productive level. These posts were held by white men from the lower classes of colonial society (Honychurch 1995: 77). Below the overseer was the slave driver. He was taken from among the slave population but held a post of responsibility and was entitled to respect from his fellow slaves. This position was always granted to a man. His duty was to maintain order among the slaves, to report on any rumours of rebellion, and to direct them at work. On larger plantations there would be more than one slave driver.

The lowest on the scale, and also the largest segment of the population on any plantation, were the slaves. The slave population on larger estates in Dominica numbered up to 300. Slaves lived in chattel houses, one-room wood and thatch structures on the outlying areas of the plantations. Each slave was allotted a small portion of land on the steeper areas of the plantation on which they were expected to grow basic provisions for themselves. Any surplus produced could be sold in the market, and some slaves were able to buy their

BOX 3.1

DOMINICA POPULATION BY STATUS, MID-EIGHTEENTH CENTURY

Year	Europeans	Free People of Color	Slaves	Total
1730	351	30	425	776
1731	432	36	565	1033
1743	717		1114	3030
1769	1718	300	5872	7980

Source: Baromé 1972: 84

freedom in this way. Besides being responsible for providing most of their own food, slaves worked long and hard hours in the fields. Slaves were divided into two general groups, field slaves who worked in gangs planting and harvesting the crops and a smaller group assigned to tasks that required more skill, usually those involved in processing the crop. On sugar plantations, for example, slaves skilled in the production of sugar and syrup from the cane plant were very important. In addition, European artisans, masons, and carpenters were also employed on the estates (Honychurch 1995: 77).

Finally, the planter or manager also lived in a large house on each estate. Domestic workers, including house slaves, cooks, and chambermaids, were employed in these tasks and had a somewhat higher status than did the field slaves. On British-owned plantations, the main house was called the "great house," on French-owned plantations it was often called "*La cou*" or the yard. It was on the lands of these plantations, mini-societies unto themselves, that the new culture was born. Before turning to a brief discussion of the new cultural forms that emerged during this era, there are two more aspects of social life that need attention, gender relations and repression.

BOX 3.2

THE CODE NOIR

Instituted in 1685 by edict of Louis XIV of France, and subsequently modified, the Code Noir defined the conditions of slavery on plantations in the French colonies. The code also restricted the activities of the Free People of Color living in French-controlled areas, for example, by forbidding certain articles of clothing and decoration. The Code also stipulated that slaves be baptized by the Roman Catholic Church and made allowances for marriage of slaves. Due to the Code Noir, and the relatively small size of the French-owned plantations in Dominica, there was some variation in experience for the slaves on these plantations compared to those on the British-owned estates.

GENDER RELATIONS ON THE PLANTATION

In his pioneering work in Caribbean feminist historiography, *Centering Women*, Hilary Beckles (1999: 3) has identified "3 historical sites where gender discourses seemed advanced and determining of social relations and popular perceptions of identity." Those were pre-colonial West Africa, the Caribbean Plantation Complex, and the global political challenge to the legitimacy of slavery in the early 19th century.

In pre-colonial West Africa, there was a marked preference for female slaves as a route to male wealth and status within a patriarchal system. In these agriculturally based economies, the planting and harvesting of crops, animal husbandry, small craft production, and domestic service were all deemed women's work and there was a corresponding preference for female slaves. (Beckles, 1999: 5) Slave owners were further entitled to rights in their female slaves' offspring, provided that their fathers were outside the sphere of political influence, further increasing the value of female slaves for the biological reproduction of the labour force.

Caribbean slavery reversed traditional West African gender orders by reversing the sex-ratio pattern, by forcing West African men into labour activities deemed by their cultures and traditions to be suitable only for women, and by subjecting them to the authority of other men (Beckles 1999: 5). To prevent rebellion, planters did institute some positions of authority for African men in the position of driver and allocated higher prestige, skilled positions to them. African women were made to work alongside the men in the fields, subjected to the same brutal corporal punishments, and defined through ideological discourses as suited only to the rigours of manual labour. In this way, African men and women were "de-gendered."

In early colonial plantation societies, the general pattern was that between 65 and 75% of all slaves shipped from West Africa were males. The Caribbean was a site that witnessed an encounter between two gender orders that were in some ways completely contradictory and in other ways completely in agreement. The European and West African gender orders differed with respect to gender roles within the sexual division of labour, but shared common gender values and attitudes with respect to masculinity and the relation of women to patriarchal power (Beckles 1999: 7).

Initially "Europeans pursued coherence in the articulation of gender representation, categories of women, and work. White women described as 'ladies' were not expected to labour in the field or perform any demeaning physical task. This was clearly a class position since the thousands of female indentured servants imported from Europe between 1624 and 1680 worked on the cotton, tobacco and sugar plantations in gangs alongside their male counterparts, as well as enslaved Africans" (Beckles 1999: 6).

By the late 17th century race began to supplant class as planters implemented a policy prohibiting the use of white women in plantation labour gangs. This initiative to isolate white women from plantation fieldwork was rooted in the social needs of white patriarchy to idealise and promote the white woman as "a symbol of white supremacy, moral authority, and sexual purity. White supremacy, white males believed, conceptually required the social isolation of all white women, irrespective of class, from intimacy with the black male in order to minimize the dread of miscegenation" (Beckles 1999: 7–8).

THE DE-GENDERING OF AFRICAN WOMEN IN THE CARIBBEAN

If a version of white femininity was being used as a "symbol of white supremacy," labour regimes on plantations were based on a discourse that shaped the "African Woman" ". . . as essentially 'non-feminine.' ". . ." Primacy was placed upon her allegedly muscular capabilities, physical strength, aggressive carriage, and sturdiness . . . she was represented as ideally suited to manual labour" (Beckles 1999: 10).

The ideological "defeminization" of the black woman also contributed to a gender order that negated black motherhood and devalued maternity. Slave owners argued that the low fertility rates found among black female slaves was further evidence of their lack of appropriate femininity. "Since it was 'natural,' they asserted, for women to desire motherhood, black women's apparent low fertility, within the context of alleged sexual promiscuity," suggested "a kind of moral underdevelopment rather than physical inability" (Beckles, 1999:11). African women who rejected the plantation's gender regime by refusing to work while pregnant or in the three months following childbirth, as was the custom in West Africa, were subject to the whip. White women, by contrast, were held up as the ideal of femininity as the following words, written by a British magistrate resident in Dominica in the late eighteenth century shows:

> . . . *[T]he generality of the English white women in the West Indies are as lovely as in any part of the world besides, make as good wives, tender mothers, and as agreeable companions. It is true they are not so remarkable for that pleasing florid complexion, which is peculiar to the sex in England; but they have in common as clear white skins, are as delicately and well featured women as in any part of creation; especially for being fine, neat workers at their needle, and making the best nurses, as well as oeconomists.*
> *Thomas Atwood 1791:211–212*

White women, whether born in the tropics or in Europe, were according to elite discourse, delicate, domestic, and docile. As this discourse began to essentialize the nature of "woman," the de-gendering of African women on the plantations became a part of the discourses of the abolitionists.

THE ABOLITIONISTS AND THE "RE-GENDERING" OF AFRICAN WOMEN IN PLANTATION SOCIETY

Abolitionists visiting plantations in the Caribbean were horrified by the "slave owners' disregard for black motherhood and maternity" (Beckles 1999: 12). These visitors carried with them a gender ideology that emphasized the need for women to be protected from male tyranny. Even those who remained in favour of the institution of slavery called for policies of reform vis a vis the treatment of female slaves. An important effect of this campaign was a reformulation of gender representations and the establishment of new, gender-based management initiatives on the plantations. African women came to be represented as members of the "gentler sex," and as such, physically inferior to men. To implement this new gender regime, planters began to import more female slaves. Policies were enacted to reduce the labour demands on pregnant and lactating women, to improve (to some extent) their material incentives (monetary rewards and improved diet), and to reduce their susceptibility to corporal punishments such as whipping. In addition, planters began to encourage Christian-style marriages and a nuclear family structure by, for instance, allowing people in such unions to remain together and live as a family. However, the new gender regime did not rely on material and living style rewards alone. "Monk" Lewis was a Jamaican planter. His comments point to a shift in the value of the institution of motherhood for African slave women, a system emphasizing their rights to honour and respect.

> *I then gave the mothers a dollar each, and told them, that for the future they might claim the same sum, in addition to their usual allowance of clothes and provisions, for every infant which should be brought to the overseer alive and well on the fourteenth day; and I also gave each mother a present of a scarlet girdle with a silver medal in the centre, telling her always to wear it on feasts and holidays, when it should entitle her to marks of peculiar respect and attention, such as being one of the first served, and receiving a larger portion than the rest; that the first fault which she might commit, should be forgiven upon production of this girdle; and that when she should have any favour to ask, she should always put round her waist, and be assured, that on seeing it the overseer would allow the wearer to be entitled to particular indulgence. On every additional child an additional medal is to be affixed on the belt, and precedence is to follow the greater number of medals. I expected that this notion of an order of honour would have been treated as completely fanciful and romantic; but to my great surprise, my manager told me, that he never knew a dollar to be better bestowed than the one which formed the medal of the girdle, and that he thought the institution likely to have a very good effect.*
> *Lewis 1929:108-9*

M.G. Lewis argued that the rearing of children, domesticity and family life exerted a steadying and maturing influence upon black women. To him, mothers appeared more moral, less sexually promiscuous, and more politically conforming (Beckles 1999: 13).

In response to the criticism of abolitionists, new gender ideologies were formulated to encourage female slaves to give birth (planters, policy makers, and moralists believed, as mentioned earlier, that black women were preventing conception or terminating pregnancies because they were hostile to motherhood in the context of slavery). Two desired outcomes of these new policies were to "naturally" increase the slave population and to counter the arguments of abolitionists and reformers that were critical of the disregard for female slaves' natural gender roles (as mothers) and femininity (as members of the "gentler sex.") New management policies called for reduced work hours for pregnant women, post-natal care for lactating women and their offspring, and protection from corporal punishment during pregnancy. Changes were also seen in slave sex ratios around this time, reflecting a new recruitment policy favouring the importation of female slaves:

> *By the middle of the 17th century, slave owners had legislated the principle of matrilineal descent in order to assure the reproduction of the slave system and ensure that only black and coloured offspring would be born into slavery. The natural reproduction of the slave population became an important, cost effective supply strategy and targeted the slave woman with a new ideological system of gender representations.*
> Beckles 1999: 8

REPRESSION

In 1804 the slaves of the French island of Haiti organized a massive and successful revolution, making Haiti the first independent black republic in the Americas. This caused an already fearful European minority to increase repressive measures against their slaves, particularly by banning drumming, religious gatherings, and other expressions of African identity on the plantations. Combined with the sexual violence experienced by slaves at the hands of their overseers and managers, these rules against self-expression contributed to the harsh conditions of slavery that make the creole cultural forms something of a miracle, for the slave population did resist and were able to retain certain aspects of their own identity in the process.

RESISTANCE

Slaves took numerous and creative steps to make life bearable. Each element of creole culture—language, dance, music, and dress is itself a miracle, for each were created under the harsh and repressive conditions of slavery.

THE GENESIS OF CREOLE CULTURES IN DOMINICA

LANGUAGE

From the description above, it should be clear that the various peoples working on the plantations came from diverse linguistic backgrounds including English, French, and a vast array of West African languages including Ibo, Yoruba, and Dahomey. Living and working together people needed to find a way to communicate with one another. Through time a new language, called Kwéyòl, was developed. Kwéyòl is the name for the creole language spoken in Dominica and other parts of the Caribbean subject to French influence or domination during the colonial period. Linguistically, creole languages are languages that were formed in situations of acculturation, when peoples from different language groups come into regular contact with one another and need to find a way to communicate. Initially, a pidgin will develop, usually with specialized terms that are necessary for the type of contact, for example words specific to trade or commerce. Through generations, a pidgin may develop into more mature creole languages with developed rules and native speakers (that is, people who learn the language as their first language of communication) (Kottak 2007: 90).

DANCE

Dominican historian Lennox Honychurch (1995: 79) records an old patois saying: *"En temps esclavage negre teyka dansé Kalanday en glacis."* This translates to "In the days of slavery, the slaves would dance on the glacis on Sundays." The glacis, recall, is the drying platform found on French-owned coffee estates. Eighteenth century artworks depicting daily scenes from Dominica provide a sense of these occasions. Two of these are reproduced in Lennox Honychurch's *The Dominica Story* and are also available for viewing on the Internet (see web-links). The men and women danced in fine, colourful clothing, dancing, drumming, or standing by and watching. The main types of dance that developed during the Plantation Era were the Quadrille and the bèlè. Historical records also contain vivid accounts of the clothing worn by slaves and Free People of Colour, and especially the dresses worn for dances and other special events.

DRESS

Whether free or enslaved, the historical records indicate that women in the Plantation Era spent a great deal of money on fine clothing and decorative jewellery. Slave women, restricted to the wearing of the plain chambray or denim outfit during the workweek, wore their finery on Sundays at the dances and social gatherings in the marketplace. Viewing the 18th century painting of

Italian artist Agostino Brunias (see web-links), one gets a sense of the flourish of the dress worn by slaves and Free People of Colour in Dominica in the late 1700s. According to Dominican author and historian Edward Scobie (1965), the "*ghip*" (also "*jip*" or "*jup*") was the first form of creole dress worn by women in Dominica. He dates the emergence of the jip, based on readings of archival sources, to 1784, or around fifty years before Emancipation. During the period of slavery, female field slaves were provided with a basic dress or covering made from a simple piece of denim or chambray fabric, which they were made to wear. Household slaves were provided with the same basic fabric, but the estate owners, and Scobie speculates more likely their wives, began to dress their domestic slaves in outfits that were simplified versions of their own elaborate European style of dress (Scobie 1965: 45).

Freed female slaves and Free Women of Colour altered the simple outfit worn by the slaves in various ways, creating more elaborate and colourful styles called the jip and *wob dwiyet* respectively. The jip comprised an ankle-length madras skirt worn with a white chemise or blouse. The outfit was finished with a madras head scarf and madras neckerchief, often matching the madras pattern of the skirt. The jip is one of the two styles of national dress worn today during Heritage Day and other national celebrations. The wob dwiyet was a more formal and elaborate dress with petticoats and brightly coloured overskirts. The 18th century historian Thomas Atwood commented:

> *The free people of color are chiefly of French extraction, and most of them came from the islands of that nation from whence they have retired on account of the severity of French laws which prohibit them from wearing shoes, stockings, ornaments of any dress after the fashion of white people. . . . Their preparations are usually very expensive; their ladies being usually dressed in silks, silk stockings and shoes; buckles, bracelets and rings of gold and silver to considerable value. . .*
>
> Atwood 1791: 212

Besides taking great care with their dress, Afro-Caribbean women of the time took strong measures to reassert their femininity and strength, as Hilary Beckles has noted. For example, slave women took on nurturing roles, caring for family members, even when separated by the practice of selling mates and offspring to other plantations, thus demonstrating their "natural" attachment to their children. This demonstrated the falsity of the white elites' assertions that African women were not appropriately maternal. Secondly, slave women took on roles that removed them from the brutalities of field labour, acting as market sellers, hucksters, and leaders in rebellions and revolutionary movements (Beckles 1999: 11). Market roles were also taken up by newly freed slaves in Dominica who "often turned to becoming retail vendors or *marchandes* for the storerooms and warehouses along the landing point or Bay Front" (Scobie 1965: 46).

Colonial discourses de-gendered and hypersexualized African bodies, while at the same time constructing white femininity and morality. These racialized discourses of gender and sexuality were used in attempts to justify the continued subjugation of persons of African and "mixed" descent. As metropolitan discourses began to essentialize gender, abolitionists used the "unnatural gender regime" found on Caribbean plantations in their debates against the immorality of slavery. Planters responded by modifying their gender regime to adapt to some of the new essentialist discourses of gender. Slave women and Free Women of Colour rejected these discourses by taking on nurturing roles, by engaging in tasks that removed them from the rigours of field work, and by donning fine clothing and dancing on the glacis on Sundays. Their dress and dances are commemorated on Heritage Day and are the subject of the next chapter.

CHAPTER **SUMMARY**

Key Terms

GENDER - Distinguishes the social significance placed upon the biological facts of being male or female within particular social contexts.

INDENTURED LABOURERS - People who had borrowed money for passage and had agreed to work off the debt during a specified period of time.

PLANTATION SOCIETY - Used to delineate the complex of economic, political, and social structures found on the plantations or estates during the era of slavery.

Discussion Questions

1. What was the general structure of plantation society?

2. What were some of the ways that the ruling class used ideas about gender and race to try to establish or legitimate the social and economic hierarchy of plantation society?

3. What were some of the differences between Dominica and other colonies during the colonial period outlined by the author?

4. In what ways did the adoption of fancy dress by slave and Free Women of Colour constitute an act of resistance? Why might some authors interpret this as accommodation or imitation?

5. What does it mean to refer to the processes of creolization and the cultural products produced through this process as a "miracle"?

WEB - LINKS

Agostino Brunias: http://www.brunias.com/wi_brunias.html

The Code Noir: http://chnm.gmu.edu/revolution/d/335/

Slavery images: http://hitchcock.itc.virginia.edu/Slavery/index.php

FURTHER READING

Beckles, Hilary McD 1999.

Centering Woman: Gender Discourses in Caribbean Slave Society. Kingston: Ian Randle, Publishers.

Gates, Henry Louis Jr. (ed) 2002.

The Classic Slave Narratives. New York: New American Library (Signet Classics).

Honychurch, Lennox 1995.

The Dominica Story: A History of the Island. London: Macmillan Caribbean.

Whitfield, Harvey Amani 2005.

From American Slaves to Nova Scotian Subjects: The Case of the Black Refugees, 1813–1840. Toronto: Pearson, Prentice Hall.

4

Performing Dominican Dances in Traditional Dress, Roseau October 1996, author's photograph.

HERITAGE DAY, CELEBRATING CREOLE CULTURAL EXPRESSIONS

CREOLE CULTURE

During the cultural season that begins in early September and ends on November 4 (Box 4.1), Dominicans celebrate the cultural traditions which emerged during the Plantation Era—the music, food, dance, and dress of the slaves and Free People of Colour. From October through to November 3 (Independence Day), restaurants feature special cuisine, and government, bank, and hotel staff dress in traditional clothing. Jing-Ping bands play on the sidewalks, dancers perform bèlè and Quadrille on the streets and on stages across the country, and people make a concerted effort to speak Kwéyòl in settings where English is the norm the rest of the year. November 4 is Community Day of Service. On this day, people around the country organize into labour groups that re-invoke the tradition of the

---

BOX 4.1

INDEPENDENCE DAY (NOVEMBER 3)

- Preparations in a selected village begin, early September
- Jing-Ping bands play around the country, beginning mid-late September
- Miss Wob Dwiyet Contest, Arawak Theatre, Roseau
- Madam Wob Dwiyet Contest, Arawak Theatre, Roseau
- Village Miss and Madam Wob Dwiyet Contests, around the country
- Dance and story telling competitions around the country
- Traditional Children's Toy and Dance Show
- Jounen Kwéyòl, Friday preceding Independence Day
- Heritage Day, Sunday preceding Independence Day
- Community Day of Service, around the country

koudmen. Like the koudmen, people work together on large jobs such as repairing a road, clearing grass and shrubs from the roadside, or cleaning beaches or large churches. The spirit is one of community and cooperation. This chapter will focus on Heritage Day, celebrated in a different village each year on the Sunday preceding Independence Day.

Heritage Day is a day specifically devoted to all of the traditions associated with the three hundred years of creolization. This chapter describes some of these traditions and relates them to the historical construction of race, gender, and sexuality of the colonial period that gave birth to these modes of dress, dances, and the creole language, the Plantation Era described in the previous chapter.

A BRIEF HISTORY OF HERITAGE DAY AND INDEPENDENCE DAY

In 1965, Dominica became a Crown Colony of Britain. The Chief Minister Honourable E. O. LeBlanc formally instituted November 3 as "Discovery Day." In a pamphlet published by the government, LeBlanc outlined the rationale behind this new holiday in Dominica:

> *The decision of the government to celebrate Discovery Day the 3rd of November as Dominica's Day stems from the growing recognition that we are members of a society that needs to rediscover its moral bearings and its sense of purpose....*
>
> *For hundreds of years we have played the role of copyist and our indigenous social structure is constantly being eroded by external influence, but at every turn we demonstrate our yearning desire to retain our own customs in preference to the imported ones which we can with the best efforts only poorly imitate....*
>
> *When we can no more feel ashamed of our patois which is so rich and romantic, when we can listen to our steel bands, our bamboo flutes and our goat skin tamboos and dance to their rhythm with pride and joy, when we can appreciate the rapture experienced by persons both young and old listening to a raconteur delivering his impromptu stories prefaced by "Messieurs Queek"*[i] *to which the audience replies "Quack" we will agree with Tennyson that "those old days had thrice the life of these"...*
>
> Chief Minister Honourable E.O. LeBlanc 1965: 5-6

"Discovery Day" became "Independence Day" in 1978, when Dominica became an independent member of the Commonwealth. The festivities first celebrated on Discovery Day in 1965 have evolved into a cultural season that stretches from September, escalating in October, and carrying through to

November 4. The spirit of intent expressed by LeBlanc in the above statement remains central to these celebrations. The need to institute official recognition and celebration of Dominican traditions stemmed from centuries of racism and colonialist attitudes that denigrated the customs of the black majority beginning with the constructions of race, class, gender, and sexuality that marked plantation society, as described above in Chapter 3. It also has formed and continues to serve as a key component in the forging of an independent Dominican national identity.

THE START OF THE SEASON – JING-PING

Dominicans know that Heritage Day is approaching, even without looking at a calendar. Sometime in September, Jing-Ping bands are heard playing throughout the countryside, in rural villages, and on street corners in town. The Jing-Ping band has a unique sound, and throughout my stay, I only heard this form of music between September and November 3 and during *séwènol* at Christmas time in the Carib Territory.[ii] The Jing-Ping band plays the music that accompanies many of the creole dances of Dominica, including quadrilles, polkas, and *mazouks* (see below). This form of music "owes its origins to the string quartets typical of Europe's eighteenth century, baroque style" (Phillip and Smith 1998: 63). Through creolization, African elements of rhythm, harmony, and melody transformed the European baroque and European-derived tunes into a form unique to Dominica. One of the main areas of transformation occurred in the instrumentation. Jing-Ping bands combine a rhythmic instrument, the *tanbal*; a bass instrument, the "boom-boom"; and a percussive instrument, the *gwaj* or *siyak*; with one or more melodic instruments, such as an accordion, bamboo flute, or harmonica.

The tanbal is a hand-held drum, 18 inches in diameter and 3 1/2 inches deep. The tanbal is made by stretching a goat skin tightly around a circular wooden frame which is lined with copper buttons. To play the instrument, one holds the drum in the crook of the left arm and uses the right hand to beat on the goat skin. The sound produced is similar to that of a tambourine. The boom-boom is typically a hollowed out piece of bamboo about 2.5 inches in diameter and 4 feet in length. The instrument produces a high or low tone that is produced by blowing into the tube. The gwaj or siyak is a tin cylinder with holes punched into its side. It measures 3 1/2 inches in diameter by 10 1/2 inches in length and resembles a kitchen grater. Hard seeds are placed inside the cylinder to produce a sound similar to a maraca. To play this instrument, a musician uses a scraper made of a piece of wood with three long wires of hard metal stuck into one end (Philip and Smith 1998: 64). The sound produced combines the scraping of the metal and rattling of the seeds. The melodic instrument most often used is the accordion which carries the tune played by the band. Jing-Ping bands provide musical accompaniment for several of Dominica's dances including the Quadrille (see below). The bands played on the streets of the capital throughout October and were a prominent feature of *Jounen Kwéyòl*, where people spoke Creole in the capital, and wore the national dress usually reserved for special performances of Quadrille and for tourist displays. This distinctive dress is described below, and is only somewhat modified from the dress described in historical accounts in Chapter 3.

DRESS: WOB DWIYET, JUP, AND NATIONAL DRESS

Traditional dress for women includes the *wob dwiyet* and madras head ties, or *jup* and white blouse. "National dress" for men includes black pants, a white shirt, and a red sash. These distinctive modes of dress date back to the Plantation Era. According to Dominican historian Lennox Honychurch, "the only way free blacks could exhibit their superiority *was to imitate the white masters to the extreme,* and one of the ways this could be done was through clothes" (Honychurch 1995: 80, emphasis added). Hilary Beckles (1999) provides an alternative interpretation with his focus on slave women's practice of buying fine fabrics and making fine dresses to wear to church and market on their one day of rest. For Beckles, this was an act of resistance against what he terms the "defeminization" of African women in plantation society. Whatever the motivation or interpretation, the record demonstrates that colourful head wraps of African inspiration were added to European dress. Later the colourful madras fabric was added, and these became the traditional jup and wob dwiyet.

Today, these styles represent resistance and creativity and emphasize the modesty and respectability of Dominican women. The women are fully covered in a long skirt or dress. Every year, women compete in the Miss Wob Dwiyet contest, which I was told repeatedly is "not a beauty contest." Contestants are judged for their ability to "wear the dwiyet." This refers to carrying the dress and petticoats with panache, the bunched fabric at the back of the dress must be swished and swirled in such a way as to emphasize the sensual body underneath the dwiyet, under cover of the appropriate modesty of the folds of fabric. During the Madam Wob Dwiyet show, older women parody this movement with exaggerated swinging of the hips and flirtatious postures.

Watching Dominican women "wear the dwiyet" I was certain that these modes of dress were more than a simple attempt to imitate the women of the planter class. They were adopted to demonstrate the dignity and respectability of peoples otherwise denied claims to these attributes by the dominant, mostly white, planter class of the colonial period. The sporting of national dress was an important part of Jounen Kwéyòl.

JOUNEN KWÉYÒL – CREOLE (LANGUAGE) DAY

Although English is Dominica's official language, Kwéyòl is the first language spoken by many Dominicans. The language has an uneasy status in Dominica. Jounen Kwéyòl, celebrated the Friday preceding Heritage Day, is a day when people dress in traditional dress, restaurants serve traditional Creole food, and people speak Kwéyòl in town (ideally) and other settings where Kwéyòl would not usually be spoken. The day marks an attempt to grant the creole language respectability, and to prevent the language from dying out. Preserving and respecting Kwéyòl are the goals of the Komité Pou Etide Kwéyòl (KEK).

It was at the initial organizational meeting for Heritage Day that I first met Marcel "Djamala" Fontaine, a founding member of Dominica's Komité Pou Etide Kwéyòl. He was wearing a t-shirt embossed with Kwéyòl words and their English translations. After finding out who he was, I asked him if he would be willing to teach me some Kwéyòl. He agreed, and just after he did so an older fisherman from Soufriere spoke some angry words to him in a fast Kwéyòl. Later Djamala told me that the man was upset with him—"why would you teach a beke [white person] our language?" he had asked. Throughout my stay I found that people had mixed feelings about Kwéyòl. "Nancy," a woman in her sixties who runs a snack shop in the capital, told me that when she was a child, her grandmother would "beat her" if she spoke to her in Kwéyòl. Other patrons in the shop quickly joined in our discussion (I had ordered my lunch in Kwéyòl, Nancy was politely telling me that I had been disrespectful). They too had been reprimanded for speaking Kwéyòl to their elders. It is precisely this attitude that the celebrations of this period seek to modify.

HERITAGE DAY 1996: SCOTTS HEAD SOUFRIERE

Pearl Christian, an officer with the Cultural Division, opened the Cultural Gala with the following remarks:

> *Jodi nou ka célébwé nou heritage. Nou ka célébwé manjé nou ka manjé. Nou ka célébwé pawol nou ka pawlé. . . . Et jodi cet yon bel jou!* (Today we are celebrating our heritage. We are celebrating the food we eat. We are celebrating the language we speak . . . and today is a beautiful day! —My translation)

Heritage Day, like the village feasts that take place throughout the year, began with a Catholic Mass. The priest marked the occasion by wearing a madras cloth chasuble over a white alb. He also said the entire mass in Kwéyòl. Throughout the congregation, women were wearing their wob dwiyet and madras head ties, or jup and white blouse, and men were dressed in business suits or in their national dress. At the mid-point of the three-hour service, women bearing baskets laden with produce and dressed in colourful jup and dwiyet ensembles entered the church. They walked, single file, down the centre aisle of the church toward the altar. Their baskets were filled with produce provided by farmers from the two villages and surrounding area. A group of young girls performed a dance. The priest blessed the baskets of fruit, vegetables, and fish that the women had laid out on the altar. With this, the work of the majority of the villagers was acknowledged and celebrated.

After mass, the congregation followed the priest; himself led by an altar boy carrying a life-sized crucifix, out into the village. In the weeks before Heritage Day, residents from Soufriere and Scotts Head had met with members of the Cultural Division to plan the displays, events, and decorations that were used for the festivities. The people decided to use fishnets, local agricultural produce, and crafts to decorate the church's interior. The planning committee was also responsible for the display that the crowd viewed after mass. Tables covered with samples of produce from the gardens of area farmers lined the room. A couple of men, one in national dress, displayed the technique for repairing fishing nets signalling the importance of fishing to this region in Dominica. Jars of guava jam, sweets, and plates of prepared food covered another table. On the back wall, various styles of coal pots,[iii] coal irons,[iv] *flès*, mortar and pestle, *kôkôt,* and calabash,[v] many on loan from residents across Dominica, were displayed as replicas of the past. Between utterances of "My grandmother had one of those, wi!" I overheard other passersby comment "But I still use that!" Again, the festivities included a commemoration of the daily lives of many Dominicans.

After viewing the displays, people were directed out to a stage (built for the occasion) outside to watch the Cultural Gala. Performers offered the audience a series of speeches, dances, and musical performances. The Roseau Cultural Group performed a Quadrille, a European-derived dance reminiscent of an English step dance involving four male-female pairs dressed in wob dwiyet and national dress. Two dance groups—one children's group, one adult—performed the bèlè. People describe this dance as an African dance, and there are five types of bèlè danced in Dominica today. In this dance, a couple dances, barefoot, to a drum and an a capella women's call and response called *la vouwé*. At an earlier event during the Creole Season (Children's Traditional Toy and Dance Show) the Master of Ceremonies described the bèlè to her audience as follows, "This is what the slaves did to make baby slaves." In contrast to the rather staid moves of the Quadrille, bèlè dancers move their hips, buttocks, and feet to the strong rhythm of the accompanying drum. Other performances included flag wavers, modern dancers, and singers. However, it was the performances of the Quadrilles and the bèlè that people described as being traditional and Dominican. I will now turn to a discussion of these major dance forms and the music that accompanies each.

CREOLE DANCE FORMS: THE QUADRILLE AND BÈLÈ

In his forward to Daryl Phillip and Gary Smith's (1998: viii) *The Heritage Dances of Dominica*, Lennox Honychurch observes:

> *The heritage dances of Dominica emerged as part of a widespread creolising process over a period of some three hundred years. It was a process of borrowing elements from two or more cultures, altering them to fit a specific historical experience and combining them to form a third culture with its own separate identity. Language was therefore encoded and experiences were transmitted in the memorised lyrics of the songs, in the steps and movements and in the music. The drum and body spoke at a time when the written word was absent.*

The specific historical experience Honychurch is referring to in the above quotation, is, as mentioned earlier, that of plantation slavery, and later, colonial Dominica. The forms of dance created during that three hundred year span included many diverse dance types, but two dances dominated the cultural performances I attended, the Quadrille and the bèlè. I will now turn to a description of each of these two creole dance forms.

THE QUADRILLE

The European-derived Quadrilles are danced throughout the French Caribbean, including Guadaloupe, Martinique, and St. Lucia, as well as in Dominica. These dance forms were introduced in the 18th and 19th centuries by French planters. Originally, the Quadrilles were reserved for the elite planter class, but today they are danced by Caribbean people from all socioeconomic classes. Indeed, for many nations in the French Caribbean, including Dominica, these dances have come to be a central aspect of national identity and source of national pride. At the same time, Quadrilles are still symbols of literacy and high social status (Cyrille 2005: 224).

Historically the Quadrille was probably first danced by slaves who worked as domestics and therefore had closer contact with the planters and their families. Records indicate that this class of slaves was taught a modified version of a Quadrille by French missionaries eager to modify their "African" movements and gestures to something more closely resembling European styles (Cyrille 2005: 225). According to ethnomusicologist and dance specialist Dominique Cyrille, dancing the Quadrille was a mark of status among the slaves and Free People of Colour. It came to be associated with proximity to the elite French population and to distinguish domestic slaves and free people from the field slaves. In Dominica the Quadrille was more likely brought to the island in the late 18th century by "poor French whites" (Phillip and Smith 1998: 15); however, French missionaries had also been on the island since the mid-17th century and there was commerce between slaves in Guadaloupe and Martinique and those living in Dominica. In any case, for all of the French islands, field slaves also danced the Quadrille. Quadrille's association with elite or European styles or perhaps its ability to facilitate the masking of African rituals and social standards meant that "quadrille dancing became a symbol of power and freedom in the French Caribbean" (Cyrilly 2005: 225).

The Quadrille is a type of square dance comprising four couples dancing in four figures or formations, each being executed according to a predetermined sequence. Phillip and Smith (1998) report that there are seven variations of the quadrille performed in Dominica, but here I will restrict my description to the basic sequence of four figures. The first of these is called the "*patalon*" and is a general introduction of the eight dancers to their audience. The dancers begin by standing across from one another and they then introduce themselves with the *avansé*—a movement that involves crossing the dance area into the center and then *dams* and *kavalyés* (women and men) exchange places using stylized flirtatious movements and gestures. The next step in the sequence is called "*La Poul*" and is decribed as "a step that represents a hen and cock in courtship" (Phillip and Smith 1998: 95). In la poul, the kavalyé and dam execute a stylized dance of flirtation while remaining apart from one another. The third figure is called "*Lété*" and involves the couples holding each other by the right hand (called "*lanman*"). Finally, there is *la trinitez*, where each kavalyé dances with two dams. For performances of the Quadrille, the men dress in national dress and the women adorn themselves in the colourful wob dwiyet.

Despite its European derivation and its role in missionary and planter attempts to repress African styles of movement and sound, the Quadrille "provided grounds for the blending of African and European traditions" (Cyrille 2005: 229). The formation and combination of specific sequences of movement resemble ritual dances derived from the Bight of Benin—one of the areas in Africa that was the original home of many of slaves brought to the French colonies during the period of slavery. Dominique Cyrille (2005: 229) hypothesizes that "the transposition of this custom in Martinique helped the masking of rituals in quadrilles. Thus, when performed by the slaves, the quadrilles . . . served to mask what, to the French, were unwelcome African customs and, paradoxically, helped to maintain them in another form in the French Caribbean." If this is true of the Quadrilles, it is unquestionably the case that the other major dance form performed in Dominica, and in the French Caribbean more generally, is more usually associated with an African past and with a refusal to accommodate European tastes—namely, the bèlè.

BÈLÈ

The African derived bèlè is performed to drumming and a call and response style of song that was once used for keeping track of significant events in the lives of family members and neighbours. Today, the bèlè is used to address issues of wider social significance (Cyrille 2005: 230). Unlike the quadrilles, bèlè is egalitarian and highly participatory in nature. "In the house yards of Dominican villages and hamlets, a bèlè dance intensifies social discourse among its participants. In so doing, the dance does much more than entertain and edify an audience. It seeks to both interpret and solidify social solidarity (Philip and Smith 1998: 32)." The bèlè performance highlights community and cooperation. Many songs that accompany the bèlè contain allusions to slavery and the African past, and indeed at national performances the dance is introduced in ways that explicitly evoke the history of slavery as we saw above.

To reiterate, while the Quadrille, with its melodic and rhythmic Jing-Ping music, highlights a modified form of European dance, the bèlè seems to be African in its rhythm and egalitarian in its ethos. Dominicans themselves emphasize the African-ness, however understood, of this dance. The comment about the dance enhancing social solidarity refers to a number of important elements. First, the dance is typically performed on the ground, alongside a potential audience rather than on a raised platform or stage. Second, the dancers wear informal, loose clothing. The dam wears a jup (skirt) with a petticoat underneath to protect her modesty when she lifts her skirt. Her blouse is loose. The kavalyé wears loose-fitting short or long pants, and may or may not wear a shirt. Both dancers are barefoot. Finally, all people present participate through both the call and response nature of the music and through calling out encouragement or criticism of the dam and kavalyé. In these ways, the separation between performers and audience is minimized. During official national performances, however, the dance is performed on stage, but even then, audience members participate with their remarks and may tap out the rhythm.

Musical accompaniment for the bèlè includes a drum, a shak-shak, and a ting-ting. The drum is carved from a hollow tree trunk or cask and a piece of goat-skin is stretched over the top of the hollow and attached at the sides by rope. Bèlè drummers, or *tanboyé* as they are called in Kwéyòl, usually make their own drums. The shak-shak is a gourd or other hollow sphere, sometimes attached to a wooden stick, filled with seeds and produces a sound like a maraca. The ting-ting is a metal triangle and stick that produces a ringing-like sound. Vocal accompaniment is provided by the lead female singer called a *chantwèl* and a chorus of two or more singers called the *lavwé*.

Participants form a circle, and this may, as mentioned above, include the "audience." The dancer's body shifts forward, the knees are usually slightly bent, and the dancers hold their arms away from their bodies. The movements are highly gendered and somewhat provocative. The man's steps are firm and heavy, the woman's light and flirtatious with a sensuous movement of her hips. Occasionally the dam will lift her skirt and shake her hips suggestively. Foot work is constant for both dancers. The bèlè and Quadrille featured prominently during the cultural gala on both Heritage Day festivities that I attended.

CONCLUSION

Once stigmatized by colonial powers and the urban elite, the wob dwiyet, bèlè, Kwéyòl and konté (story-telling) that developed during the Plantation Era are celebrated with pride during the festivals leading up to Independence Day. Products of creolization and hybridization, or cultural interchange, these traditions cannot be read as mere imitations of European customs (as in Honychurch). They do not represent a form of accommodation (as in Wilson 1973). Nor do they constitute unambiguous examples of resistance (as in Beckles 1999).

The performances that surround Independence Day serve as a reminder of the pride, dignity, and humanity of Dominican society's forebears. This is especially evidenced in the cultural gala, the central event of Heritage Day. Cultural interaction (creolization) is present in the language, dress, and many of the traditional dances. The traditions challenge the authoritative voice of the plantocracy who tried to deny the humanity of the slave population while denigrating and exploiting them. In each dance step and with each sashay of the wob dwiyet, Dominicans seem to assert their humanity and dignity and pride in their survival and the culture they created under the harsh conditions of slavery. Carnival, the subject of the next chapter, celebrates Emancipation and provides a space for the negotiation of hybridization and Dominican identity today.

CHAPTER **SUMMARY**

Key Terms

BÈLÈ - An African-dervied style of dance that is performed to the accompaniment of drums and call and response style singing.

CALL AND RESPONSE - A style of music that features a lead singer who calls out a chorus to which other singers respond.

ETHNOMUSICOLOGY - The study of social, cultural, and historical aspects of music and dance, usually focusing on the performance types specific to a particular group of people or region.

JUP - A traditional style of dress worn by women that features a madras skirt and is worn with a white blouse and madras neck and head wrap.

QUADRILLE - A European-derived style of dance that is performed by four couples and features a set sequence of steps.

WOB DWIYET - A traditional style of dress worn by women that features a full-length dress and several petticoats and is worn with a madras head wrap. The dress overlay is a brightly coloured cotton fabric, often in a madras pattern.

Discussion Questions

1. Why was Heritage Day started?

2. In what ways did the dance forms, especially the Quadrilles and bèlè, enable African-descended people to retain, if in a modified form, the traditions of their ancestors?

3. Why is the bèlè considered more egalitarian than the Quadrille?

4. What are some of the social functions of dance and music?

WEB - LINKS

Dominica Overseas National Association Quadrille Dancers 14th June 2008
http://www.youtube.com/watch?v=Jp_LuCdSH7k&feature=related

Quadrille: An American Ballroom Companion, Library of Congress
http://www.youtube.com/watch?v=3JPrMGiGJdo

Quadrille from St. Lucia
http://www.youtube.com/watch?v=hh6cWrA2DKg&feature=related

FURTHER **READING**

Manuel, Peter with Kenneth Bilby and Michael Largey 1995.

Caribbean Currents: Caribbean Music from Rumba to Reggae. Philadelphia: Temple University Press.

Sloat, Susanna (ed.) 2005.

Caribbean Dance from Abakua to Zouk: How Movement Shapes Identity. Florida: University Press of Florida.

NOTES

[i] The art of storytelling is called *konté*. The narrator signals the story is about to begin by calling out, "Messieurs Kwik!" The audience replies "Messieurs Kwak!" And the story begins.

[ii] Jing-Ping is related to the "scratch bands" of neighbouring islands, but is considered uniquely Dominican (See Phillip and Smith 1998: 61, for example).

[iii] A coal pot is a cooking vessel that uses charcoal to cook food.

[iv] A coal iron is a metal iron that is heated with charcoal and then used to press clothing.

[v] A calabash is a vessel, used as a bowl or cup, made from the shell of the fruit of the calabash tree.

A BRIEF HISTORY OF CARNIVAL

Carnival season begins December 26, when Calypsonians begin to perform entries for the Calypso Monarch competitions. From village to village the *lapo kabwit* bands begin to rehearse, their distinctive sound attracting revellers who "jump and chip"[i] behind them as they make their way along the main roads in villages around the island. As the dates for Carnival draw near, organised shows and competitions fill up the calendar—the quarter and semi-finals and the Calypso Monarch competition, The Traditional Mas show, and the Carnival Queen contest (see Box 5.1). Carnival itself begins with Jouvert Morning, shortly after midnight on the Monday before Ash Wednesday. This fête features men and women wearing inside-out pyjamas and cross-dressers, revelling in the streets to the sounds of the lapo kabwit bands. Carnival Monday and Tuesday feature parades during the day, and "jumping" or "chipping" behind trucks bearing speakers or the lapo kabwit bands playing the winning calypsos for the year throughout the night. The competitions for the Carnival monarchs that are the focus of this chapter must be understood within the wider context of Carnival.

Dominican historian and anthropologist Lennox Honychurch provides a brief account of the historical shifts and transformations of Dominica's Carnival. Carnival, or masquerade as it was more commonly called in Dominica, was initially a strongly Afro-French festival. The observance of two days of feasting before Lent has a long tradition in European Roman Catholic history and was brought to the island by the French settlers (Honychurch 1995: 167–8). The French plantocracy would don colourful masks and visit each other for vast creole fêtes from Samedi Gras through J'Ouvert to Mardi Gras. The slaves would dance outside on the glacis, a platform for the drying of the coffee beans grown on the French plantations in Dominica, or work indoors playing music, serving or entertaining the French revellers for tips (ibid). With emancipation, the freed people brought the festival from the estate onto the streets. In the two main towns, Roseau and Portsmouth, labourers, fishermen, and domestics were joined by bands from nearby villages "to flout and tear down the standards of the upper class." The themes of the *chanté mas*, songs that exposed in graphic detail scandalous events in the lives of prominent members of society, made this clear

> BOX 5.1
>
> # CARNIVAL (MONDAY AND TUESDAY PRECEDING ASH WEDNESDAY)
>
> - Calypso Monarch Competitions - Biweekly tents begin December 26
> - Calypso Monarch Finals - Saturday night preceding Carnival, Festival City, Roseau
> - Carnival Queen Competition - Friday night preceding Carnival, Festival City, Roseau
> - Traditional Mas and Pappy Show - Thursday night preceding Carnival
> - Lapo Kabwit Bands - play in villages beginning December 26
> - Jouvert Morning - Sunday, around midnight, unofficial opening of Carnival
>
> Source: Fieldnotes.

enough (Honychurch 1995: 167–8). The parade of gangs and parade of bands feature elaborate costumes:

> *Many of the costumes were unaltered from those used in tribal festivals of Central African kingdoms. The sensay outfits with cow horns were the most obvious. Rope sensay, pai fig, cloth and paper sensay were worn by the notorious bande mauvais who clashed in great street battles either with each other or the police.*
>
> Honychurch 1995: 168–9

Carnival, like the traditions described in Chapters 3 and 4, emerged through a process of hybridization. It blended European and African traditions. Carnival was a "revolt of the Dominican masses against a society which, for the rest of the year demanded their obedience" (Honychurch 1995: 167).

Sensay costumes (pictured below) were banned in 1963 and had just been reinstated as a part of Carnival in 1997, the year I was there. To the traditional

Source: Sensay dancing in the Parade of Gangs. Roseau, February 1997. Author's photograph.

rope, dried banana leaf, paper, and cloth sensay were added costumes made of flour sacks, pieces of coloured fabric, shredded pop-cans, and strips of multi-coloured rubber cut from the soles of sandals. The sensay were registered with the police (identified by a numbered tag around their necks) and not permitted to carry the traditional weapons (a stick or a cutlass).[ii] Instead, they walked empty-handed or carried more modern "weapons," for example a brief case or tennis racket. The chanté mas has been replaced by calypso music and the character of Dominica's carnival is now more reminiscent of the European-style festival, with queens, shows, and organisation (cf Honychurch 1995: 168). The spirit of the chanté mas, however, remains in the content of Dominican calypso.

CARNIVAL IN DOMINICA—1997
CALYPSO: MASKING AND DOUBLE-VOICED "CHANTING DOWN"

The Calypso Monarch Competition is one of the main events preceding Carnival. Weekly contests begin on December 26 and culminate with the Calypso Monarch Show held at Festival City (formerly Carnival City) on the

Saturday preceding Carnival. There are two calypso tents; one holds a weekly show on Wednesday evenings, the other on Friday evenings. The winner is crowned Calypso King (or Queen). Each entrant performs at least one original song, and the most popular of these receive continual airplay on Dominica's two radio stations. The winner's song becomes the main song for the road marches during the parades. In Dominica, calypsonians occasionally write humorous songs, but tend to prefer songs that contain some form of social commentary. For example, the previous January one of calypsonian de Hurricane's songs *"pou Yon Copper"* lamented that "For one piece of copper you want to rip the belly up," a protest against government negotiations with Broken Hill Properties, a mining outfit that had expressed interest in exploring Dominica's mineral resources.

Another term for this form of "social commentary" is "Chanting down" a more clear reference to the prior tradition of chanté mas, songs whose lyrics graphically exposed the scandals of members of the ruling class.

The "Traditional Mas" show, which was held at Carnival City (now Festival City) on the Thursday prior to the Queen competition, was another space where the original confrontational nature of Carnival was displayed in the "Pappy Show Wedding". This comedic performance satirized the activities of Kentucky Fried Chicken, Broken Hill Properties, the Commonwealth Development Corporation, and the government.[iii] Tearing down the "powers that be" remains a salient feature of Dominican Carnival. It is a primary feature of the calypsos (in 1997 26 of the 35 songs entered in the calypso contests explicitly or subtly criticised government and big business). The Queen competition, however, seemed to be more of a space for the celebration, assertion, and assessment of an idealised Dominican national identity, a "third space."

DOMINICA'S CARNIVAL QUEEN COMPETITION AS A "THIRD SPACE"

The positive feature of hybridity is that it invariably acknowledges that identity is constructed through a negotiation of difference, and that the presence of fissures, gaps and contradictions is not necessarily a sign of failure. In its most radical form, the concept also stresses that identity is not the combination, accumulation or synthesis of various components, but an energy field of different forces. Hybridity is not confined to a cataloging of difference. Its 'unity' is not found in the sum of its parts, but emerges from the process of opening what Homi Bhabha has called a third space within which other elements encounter and transform each other.

Papastergiadis 1997: 273

This section of the chapter describes the performance of the winning contestant in the 1997 Dominica Carnival Queen Pageant. The performance demonstrates the negotiation of hybridization in a "third space." The Carnival Queen Pageant is a competitive show where women from six of Dominica's regions compete for the title of Carnival Queen. Contestants are judged for beauty and grace (evening wear and swimsuit categories), for intelligence (a social conscience question), for the design of their costume (elaborate floats), and for their talent. The talent and costume designs of all six contestants made explicit reference to Dominica's cultural heritage, geographical location, or "spirit."

Various corporations operating in Dominica in 1997 sponsored five of the six contestants; the Carnival Development Committee sponsored the sixth. The first contestant sponsored by Dominica Beverages and Brewery (a German held corporation) entitled her performance "Mother Africa." The stage was dressed with grass huts and drums, the music in the background was heavily inflected with African-sounding drum rhythms, she wore a colourful wrap and head dress, had painted one arm black, and cried for her lost mother, Africa. Her red, green, and gold costume was titled "Cry Freedom." Contestant number 2 performed a vaudeville-style skit that will be described below. Her costume featured a parrot headdress and flowers that grow in Dominica. The third entrant, sponsored by Courts, a Caribbean-wide furniture and electronics store, performed a song she had written called "One People"—"Negro or Carib Indian We are all Dominican, One people in unity and freedom." Her costume was titled "Anthurium Garden" and featured beautifully crafted anthurium lilies in a cloud around her. The fourth performer, sponsored by a Bajan insurance company, came onto the stage dressed as an angel in a long white gown with white gossamer wings. Her performance titled, "Dare to Dream," began with a take-off of Martin Luther King's famous "I have a dream" speech. "I had a dream, Negro, Indian, Amerindian, Dark and Light, French, English and Dutch. All people. All islands were but one nation, one voice, one flag and one government. Union of the Caribbean States. Just last month Barbados chose Chiquita bananas over ours. That really hurt." Her costume entry was titled "Caribbean Queen." Contestant number 5 offered an original song, "There is a woman I know, Waitukubuli, bouyon, Calypso, prettiest thing I've ever seen. . . ." Contestant number 6, sponsored by the Carnival Development Committee (CDC) came on stage to the music of the South African band, Lady Mombassa. She dedicated her performance on the steel pan drums to a recently deceased and well-loved Dominican pan player. Before playing her drum solo (three Dominican songs) she referred to the beauty of the instrument and its melody, "the spirit of who we are . . . naturally." She sang a few lines a cappella and then began to play the drums.

Together these performances present a celebration of African heritage, location in the Caribbean region, a special pride in the beauty of "Nature Island," a reminder to respect and appreciate that beauty, and a linking of a cultural and spiritual essence that is firmly rooted in locale. The next section of this chapter discusses the vaudeville-style performance offered by Jenny Joseph[iv] (Contestant 2). This skit explicitly refers to Dominica as "a real bouyon" and traces the history of the island's inhabitants from pre-colonial times through the various stages of colonial control and contemporary times. Here is a description of the performance, entitled *The Dominica Story,* by Jenny Joseph.

> The stage was furnished with a few simple props, an easel board with a series of large cards, a suitcase with costume changes. "A keyboard player provides music. Jenny comes out onto the stage dressed in a black workout outfit cinched at the waist with a belt. Her hair is held back with a gold lamé headband and she is carrying a large suitcase. "Ladies and Gentlemen, the Dominica Story. First Arrivals (flips card) The Arawaks." Running over to the suitcase, she puts a few feathers in her hair and an oar in her right hand while making some vaudevillian-style comment. She continues to run back and forth, turning cards and changing costumes, to depict other peoples that have inhabited the island, in chronological sequence: "The Caribs;" the Spanish are introduced with a paper boat hat, a paper telescope, and the announcement "Ladies and Gentlemen, Christopher Columbus."
>
> *Land Ho! Land Ho!*
> *It's a'mine, all mine!*
> *Enrico, come here, look, land.*
> *By the way, what day is it today?*
> *Domingo? Okay we're gonna call*
> *thata one Dominica.*
> *Mama Mia, Isabela*
> *she gonna give me*
> *something good for this one!*
>
> Next come the French missionaries, represented by a black cap, a large crucifix around her neck, and a loaf of French bread. They are followed by the British, who "never did much for the island anyway." Finally, Jenny moves to "modern times," poking fun at the Taiwanese immigrants who had come to Dominica in the 1990s, and the tourists, who are introduced to a musical chorus of "Yankee Doodle" and signified by the donning of a straw hat and sunglasses. Finally, Jenny changes into a Dominican madras fabric and asks, *But seriously, I have a question. Who are we? Really? Are we Carib? Are we British? Are we French? Are we American? Let me tell you, Dominica is a real BOUYON! Hit it CK.*

At this point, the music switches to stereo and we hear a chorus of WCK's "Bouyon."

The performance ended with an explicit expression of Dominican values, an incorporation and exclusion of the various ethnicities encountered through historical interactions up to the present day. In this parody of Dominica's history, various colonial (and "post-colonial") powers are parodied as greedy, shallow, and self-interested. These characteristics are portrayed as contrary to an idealised version of Dominican national character. It is this that made the performance so successful, the story was told in a way that appealed to key elements of an idealised Dominican identity: sharing; friendliness; honesty; not greedy for money, wealth, or power; and respectful of nature, other people's property, and other people's dignity. In the performance, each of the former colonial powers (Spain, France, and Britain) was acknowledged as a part of Dominica's "bouyon," yet each was also implicitly rejected on essentially moral grounds.

CONCLUSION

> *What is evident, then, is that hybridity, much like contemporary religious syncretism, is a collective condition perceived by actors themselves to be potentially threatening to their sense of moral integrity, and hence subject to argument, reflection and contestation: a highly politicised form . . .*
>
> Werbner 1997: 12

The skit described above represents a conscious hybrid, a performance re-enacting several such moments of encounter and an effort at negotiating difference and maintaining a unity marked by moral precepts. While certain "encounters" are beyond the control of many Dominican citizens, their own moral comportment remains an arena which is firmly in their control and which is one that they guard jealously.

Carnival is, and always has been, a "hybrid" festival, one that has experienced transformations along with shifts in the socio-political landscape. Today it is, in addition to the "upside-down" world of Jouvert Morning, a third space for working through the processes of hybridization in Dominican life. Carnival provides an arena where participants and performers (the two are not always so neatly separable) work through and take control of aspects of social change and transformations that might otherwise be largely outside of their control. The sensay costumes and lapo kabwit bands of African origin, the European festival and timing, and the uniquely Caribbean creole aspects of carnival are recombined and incorporate new elements, such as the American cartoon characters, the tennis racket, the banana bags instead of banana leafs. Through the Pappy Show Wedding, calypso lyrics, and talent entries during the Queen Contest, people reflect, critique, incorporate, or reject. The general population may not, for example, be able to prevent the arrival of tourists, foreign investors, and satellite television (nor indeed do they necessarily want to stop these things) but they can attempt to control the impact of these external forces on their senses of identity. Dominicans attempt to assert control, particularly in terms of moral agency and, ultimately, selecting the best, the most "nutritive," for Dominica's bouyon. The Carnival Queen competition show described in this chapter can be understood as a site of cultural production which includes aspects of Dominica's past and present, commentaries on the various components of the "bouyon," and a statement about the moral aspects of Dominican identity. The latter was suggested through the depiction not so much of "who we are" as a satire of "who we are not." Dominican standards of moral comportment are further examined in Chapter 6.

CHAPTER **SUMMARY**

Key Terms

LAPO KABWIT BAND - Literally, "goat-skin drum" band. These bands are heard around the country during the season of Carnival and accompany groups of revelers during parades. The bands also incorporate a conch shell.

SENSAY - A traditional style of dress worn by revelers during carnival in Dominica. The costume covers the entire face and body and is made using a variety of material including paper mache, strips of fabric, dried banana leaves, and shredded pop cans, for example.

Discussion Questions

1. What are some of the main events included in the celebration of Carnival in Dominica?

2. What do the Pappy Show Wedding and Calypso have in common?

3. What are some of the social functions of carnival?

WEB-**LINKS**

Dominica Carnival 2008

http://www.dominicacarnival.com/

NOTES

[i] To "jump" is to jump and push other revellers, in time to the music, and usually in response to a lyric, e.g., "Jump up and wave." To "chip" is to shuffle your feet to the music, sometimes walking behind the band or while watching from the side of the road.

[ii] My observations here are limited to Carnival in Roseau, the capital. I heard accounts from others who had spent Carnival in Grand Bay (Sout City) and St. Joseph where the traditional weapons were in hand. I was also "accosted" by a Sensay with a cutlass in Colihaut the following year. The tradition is that the Sensay will approach with weapon raised and demand money. I gave the person a dollar, much to the chagrin of the bus driver.

[iii] British-owned Commonwealth Development Corporation had just purchased 73 per cent of Dominica Electricity Corporation in January 1997. This move was heavily criticized because the cost of electricity was expected to rise 15% and the electricity had been taken out of the hands of the British by Eugenia Charles after Hurricane David when the owners refused to make repairs and restore electricity in a timely fashion. Broken Hills Mining is a New Zealand-based mining outfit that was proposing to engage in exploratory mining in the Northeast of Dominica, another widely unpopular venture which never transpired. KFC had just opened an outlet in the capital on January 3, 1997. I cannot say that this was unpopular; the line-up stretched longer than a city block, but there were of course those who would prefer to keep chains like KFC out of Dominica.

[iv] It is usual anthropological practice to use pseudonyms, and I have done so in this case after much reflection. On the one hand, this was a public performance and the author/performer showed a great deal of ingenuity and creativity in her rendering of Dominican history. On the other hand, I do not have explicit permission to use her name and want to avoid bringing her unwanted attention. In the end, I followed the ethical guidelines provided by the American Anthropological Association.

FOLKLORE, GREETINGS, AND MORALITY IN DOMINICA

> *As soon as I desire I am asking to be considered. I am not merely here-and-now, sealed into thingness. I am for somewhere else and for something else. I demand that notice be taken of my negating activity insofar as I do battle for the creation of a human world – that is a world of reciprocal recognitions.*
> **Frantz Fanon 1986: 218**

As part of the original fieldwork that informs this ethnography, I participated in several of the activities organized by the now disbanded Movement for Cultural Awareness (MCA). For several months beginning in October 1996 I attended workshops led by MCA involving youth groups. At our weekly meeting at the Town Youth Centre on the Thursday after Carnival, Marcia and Brown, members of MCA, led the participants in a discussion about the significance of Carnival. A few weeks earlier, "Mrs. Smith," a prominent youth worker and community member, had visited as a guest speaker. Today the discussion moved from a narrative recounting of Mrs. Smith's talk to a conversation about recent shifts in the meaning of Carnival in Dominica and changes in societal attitudes more generally. The discussion quickly moved to Dominican "traditions," participants shared stories about *mous* (genies), *soucouyants* (witch/vampires), and *louga'ou* (werewolves). The content of these stories will be elaborated below. Each story, I will suggest, is best understood as a parable or morality tale, a narrative that tells us how to behave and what might happen to us if we fail to behave appropriately. The stories caution against social isolation, greed, or jealousy. Each also therefore emphasises the importance of social life, and of generous attitudes towards other members of the community. Beliefs about soucouyants, louga'ou, and mous are becoming less common (one man told me that these creatures do not like the scent of gasoline and, now that there are now more roads there are fewer soucouyants in Dominica). Although fewer people seem to believe in the actual existence of mous and soucouyant, the stories still circulate widely and they carry important messages about moral comportment—that is, about what is considered good and proper behaviour—in Dominica.

This chapter recounts these stories and describes local greeting protocols to demonstrate the connections between history, economy, gender, and moral personhood in Dominica in order to provide a deeper analysis of creole culture. The stories and assessments of daily comportment, for example, how one greets or fails to greet another person on the street, suggests that creolization and the historical experience of slavery has resulted in a value orientation based on mutual recognition and respect and an aversion to greed and power over others. While this argument is not entirely new (for example, it resonates with what Paul Gilroy has referred to as a "double-consciousness") there are strong reasons to suggest that this is an important aspect of creole culture, and certainly one that many Dominicans value as part of what it means to be Dominican. Many Dominican people restrict their involvement with the cash economy. This is not always by choice, but, for some people, it enables a degree of economic independence that some Dominicans explicitly refer to as "consciousness." Economic self-sufficiency, vis-à-vis the global capital marketplace, requires mutual cooperation. Mutual recognition, as in greeting protocols, reflects and reinforces the ethos of cooperation. The practice of the koudmen (co-operative labour exchange, revived as we saw in Chapter 4 on Community Day of Service) and women's participation in economic and community networks further ensure the realization of this ideal. Female gender roles reinforce this cooperation by blurring the distinction between "public" and "private" domains, extending the notion of family to encompass the entire community and even the nation.

The chapter begins with a discussion and analysis of a series of parables shared by the young participants and Brown that afternoon. These are then compared to greeting protocols in Dominica. The chapter then discusses the value placed on *making* rather than *buying* things, as in the higher value placed on home-made drums for musicians in both the Jing-Ping and lapo kabwit bands discussed in Chapters 4 and 5. Hegel's Master/Slave dialectic has been reworked by scholars like Paul Gilroy (1993) and Hans Georg Gadamer (1982) in ways that allow us to relate it the value orientation suggested by the ethnographic material in this chapter. Hegel's dialectic states that a person can realize a truly free self-consciousness through the reciprocal recognition of others and the fashioning of objects. Making things allows one to realize one's ability to create material objects that both prove one's being as a "mind for itself" and by creating objects that will survive after one's death. While it is not my intention to suggest that Dominicans are all Hegelians, there are some parallels between this part of Hegel's philosophy and the fundamental features of these stories and practices. In Dominica, where most people have limited access to consumer goods due to a lack of cash income, people must make their own things, but, many Dominicans explicitly refer to this practice as "consciousness." As access to consumer goods increases, people become increasingly dependent on the market economy. This creates anxiety, particularly in the climate of uncertainty brought on by the United States Trade Representative's challenge to the Lomé Convention that is currently threatening income, and structural adjustment programs that are increasing the need for cash. The social and economic changes experienced on the island in the last decade will be the subject of Chapter 7. In this chapter, we will look more closely at this notion of "consciousness" and proper or good behaviour as expressed in the stories told at the Town Youth Centre and elsewhere throughout the country, beginning with the story of the mous.

THE MOUS, A PARABLE

A mous is a kind of genie or demon that people create. The process begins when a person incubates an egg under his or her arm for 40 days. During this period, the individual must avoid contact with others. The 40-day period of incubation must end on Good Friday. At the meeting at the youth centre, Brown opened with, "Now there is the mous," and several of youth cried out, "That one is true!" and "Donald" added, "A man [who lived] by 'Marigold' made one and he threw it in the sea." I had heard the story of the mous some months earlier, when "Marvin," a friend and interlocutor, gave me an extended description during an interview in October 1996. At that time, Marvin explained the process for creating a mous in some detail, emphasizing that at the end of the incubation period, and, "I mean before midnight, you've got to keep saying *'mwen se met'w'* which means 'I am your master.'" If all goes well, the mous will hatch and although Marvin had never actually seen a mous, he explained that it was very small and "something like a genie." Like a genie, the mous would have to grant the wishes of its creator. Marvin's account emphasized that a person who made a mous would most likely ask for riches and wealth. When I asked him why more people did not go and create mous for themselves he looked alarmed and explained that most Dominicans find the mous a "very scary thing" and speculated that only someone very desperate for money might be tempted but added that "most Dominicans don't behave in this way."

One of the reasons that the mous is "a scary thing" is that there are several ways that a mous can turn, making its creator the slave. When describing a turned mous, Marvin used the word "demon." The two most common ways a mous will turn are failing to say "I am your master" first and feeding it too much. In the first case, the mous enslaved the maker right away, in the second case, it seems, the mous' appetite would be awakened. In either case, a mous that had turned would force you to do its bidding and would want to engage in sexual relations with your wife, your parents, and any other people you were close to. A turned mous, would in effect, become the master and, ". . . then you are its slave. Anything it wants you have to get it. You have to grant it its wish, cause if not it's going to abuse you and beat you. It will make your life miserable and then you might just think of dying and commit suicide yourself."

In this story, the mous seems to embody greed, and is described as a demon, in other words, the story literally demonizes greed. The language of the story, "I am your master," if it turns then "you are its slave," seems to evoke memories of slavery, a system that existed to enrich a small group of people at the expense of another group. The description of the turned mous, "It will make your life miserable and then you might just think of dying and commit suicide yourself," and its sexual appetite also evoke memories of slavery, where corporal punishment and rape were a part of the daily lives of slaves (see Chapter 3 and also Gates 2002). The story evokes memories and is also a morality tale cautioning against greed[i].

Both Brown and Marvin provided examples of men who were reputed to have had a mous. These "real life" stories shared some basic features. A person, always in these stories a man, had started out life poor. Suddenly, and with little apparent effort, the individual became excessively wealthy. In some accounts, the man also had "more than thirty children," suggesting sexual excess as well. In these cases, the person eventually came to ruin through bankruptcy, loss of friends, and loss of health. When I asked Marvin how someone would get to know that a person had a mous, he was not too sure. He speculated that the individual would have to have told someone, or perhaps be seen with one, and eventually someone would get to know, especially once the mous had turned. It seemed to me, however, that the point of the story was that one way or another, eventually the mous was bound to turn and make the owner's life miserable. Perhaps this is why stories about the mous always seemed to include instructions for destroying them. To destroy a mous, "you've got to get a boat right out in the ocean very, very far and then you take the thing, which is the mous, and you throw it behind your back and then you head straight for shore, no turning back." The mous will try to trick a person into turning back by making strange noises. These strange sounds will make it seem as though "the most scary thing is right behind you, but the most important thing, you don't turn back 'cause if you do you're dead."

MOUS AND THE MEMORY OF SLAVERY

If you turn back, the mous will kill you, take the boat, and row to shore where it will lie in wait, enslaving the next person who chances upon his path. By creating a mous then, a person places him or herself in danger. Perhaps more importantly, the person also jeopardizes spouse, family, and ultimately the entire community.

As we have seen in earlier chapters, Kwéyòl, bèlè, Jing-Ping and other elements of creole dance and music were seen as inferior by urban elites in Dominica until after 1965, in part because they were associated with slavery and with rural life. Since 1965, creole culture has come to be celebrated as part of an assertion of a uniquely Dominican national identity. The celebration of creole culture is particularly highlighted during the many events that take place around Independence Day, including Heritage Day. But, although creolization and creole culture are celebrated at this time, in all of the events I went to over the years slavery was mentioned only once. Likewise, Carnival, which as we saw in Chapter 5 is explicitly described as a celebration of freedom, slavery is rarely mentioned. In short, the memory of slavery in Dominica is often muted. Yet in the story of the mous it is explicitly retained along with an injunction to forget: "the most scary thing is right behind you, but the most important thing, you don't turn back." The mous also exhibits inappropriate sexual appetites (wants your wife, your parents, whatever woman you have). In addition, the mous is a parable about greed. In this story, the desire for wealth becomes a destructive and divisive force. Finally, it is also a story about anti-social behaviour; to make a mous a person must avoid contact with others for a period of 21 or 40 days. Withdrawing from interaction with others is, in the Dominican moral landscape, itself a highly immoral and potentially destructive act. Withdrawing from social interaction is associated with evil in other Dominican stories, including two male/female pairs—the soucouyant and louga'ou and the dyabess and dyab. Not all Dominicans believe in or talk about the mous or other similar entities (I did not encounter anyone who was not familiar with these stories). A far greater portion of the population adheres to local greeting protocols.

GREETING PROTOCOLS, "BEVERLY HILLS" AND "NASTY GIRLS"

For all its conspicuous masculinism and Eurocentrism, Hegel's allegory is relational. It can be used to point out the value of incorporating the problem of subject formation into both epistemology and political practice.

Gilroy 1992

The first part of Hegel's master/slave dialectic is relational. True self-consciousness depends upon the recognition of other self-consciousness and an awareness of the reciprocal nature of that mutual interdependence. An awareness of self in relation to others as an interdependent member of a community of self-consciousness is an essential step in the attainment of an independent self-consciousness. Most Dominicans maintain an ideal of moral comportment that resonates with Hegel's ideas about reciprocal recognition, as I suggest their almost formulaic greeting protocols reveal. Hans-Georg Gadamer has made this point, also using greeting protocols as an example of what he terms "a trivial form of recognition," by pointing to the "feeling of humiliation when a greeting is not returned," for self-awareness, as with Hegel's allegory, "reciprocity is that essential" (Gadamer 1971: 64).

In Dominica, observing greeting protocols is a central way to demonstrate that you are a decent and proper person. These protocols are not in any way trivial. They are, at heart, a basic acknowledgement of others, and failure to comply raises questions about a person's overall character and decency. In extreme cases a person's humanity may also be brought into question (as we will see with stories about soucouyant and lou'ga'ou). Standard greetings range in degree of formality, and the selection of the appropriate greeting is related to the degree of closeness, or the type of relationship, between the people engaging in the exchange. The most formal greeting, for example, is "Good Morning" or "Good Afternoon," and is the appropriate choice for a younger person addressing a senior person, usually with a "Miss" or "Mister" if the person's name is known. This would also be an appropriate greeting to use with a person whom one does not know very well. The less formal "*Sa ka fet?* (What's happening)," "*Mwen la* (I'm there)," "Okay?" "All right?" "Okay," and the Rastafarian "Yes Ras." "Yes I," "Irie? (Happy, good)," "I cool" are popular with younger people, especially young men, and are appropriate choices for greeting close friends or peers. Where possible, closer relationships also call for stopping a while to chat, but acknowledging neighbors and acquaintances as you pass them on the road is always mandatory. Bus drivers, if unable to call out, flash their headlights in greeting. For a closer friend they will, if possible, stop on the road and chat a while, tying up traffic but no one seems to mind (except tourists and expatriates). As mentioned above, failure to follow these protocols, or failure to acknowledge other people, leads to questions about a person's overall moral character.

Dominican culture generally discourages greed, selfishness, conspicuous consumption, and accumulation. Sometimes, ostentatious displays of wealth are considered a sign of immorality. For example, there is a village populated exclusively by wealthy individuals and their families, which non-residents call "Bourgeoisville" or "Beverly Hills." Describing this area in Dominica to me one day, my friend added, "Imagine Dee, they don't even say 'Good Morning' to one another!" She continued to lament that the residents of this village would "pass each other straight." Greeting protocols in Dominica are, for most people, an essential element in proper moral comportment. Greeting neighbours, and even strangers, as you pass each other on the street is an important way of displaying manners and propriety. Many older people lamented that "Children are not showing proper respect today. In my day, you would never pass an elder without saying 'Good Morning' or 'Good Afternoon.'"

One afternoon I was sitting by the bay front with two souvenir vendors, "Nora" and "Serene." A group of four tourists passed by and Nora called out, "Good afternoon. Would you care to buy something local?" The tourists did not even look in our direction, and Nora spat out, "SAVAGES!" She and Serene began a long diatribe about the ill manners of tourists and other foreigners, whom they described as "troublesome." After a while I asked, "But I'm a foreigner, no?" "Oh no, Dee, you know how it is. You are welcome here anytime" was their response.

Throughout the period of this study, people frequently made comments linking greeting protocols to moral personhood. "Lisa" was telling me about a woman of ill repute who lived near her home. "That girl will pass me on the street and when I say 'good afternoon' to her, she won't even answer. I tell you, that girl is really nasty." In Dominican English, "nasty" refers to sexual licentiousness. People link greeting protocols to class, gender, and sexuality and use them to make moral evaluations about a person's social worth. A woman who would "pass you straight" is also a woman who has a reputation for sexual promiscuity. "She has one man coming in the front door while the other is leaving through the back." People who do not follow basic greeting protocols find their very morality called into question. Consciousness, "knowing how it is," is an important aspect of moral personhood. Further evidence of the importance of sociability lies in two other morality tales that circulate in Dominica. These are the stories about creatures paired in female and male forms—the soucouyant and louga'ou, and the dyabess and dyab.

SHAPE CHANGERS

Soucouyants and Louga'ou are shape changers; human by day, they turn into dangerous supernatural beings at night. A soucouyant is a woman who sheds her skin at night and, from her breasts (nipples I think) turns into a ball of flame. One widespread story about a woman who was a soucouyant recounts how one night she flew to England. While there, she stole the queen's dress, which she wore to church the next day. The priest, speaking in creole, told the woman that she was a thief and a soucouyant. He ordered her out of the church.[ii] I heard this story three times, in three separate villages, and each time I was also shown the home of the woman (herself now deceased) and warned against associating with her descendants. In their more general manifestation, soucouyants fly around on brooms and enter their victims' homes through cracks under the door or through the window. Once inside, the soucouyant attacks her sleeping victim by biting and sucking the person's blood. At first, the victim will grow pale and tired, and if the soucouyant continues her nightly visits, the victim will die. When "Christine," a friend of mine, was telling a group of us that there are several soucouyants in her natal village, I asked her "How do you know a woman is a soucouyant?" "It's easy," she assured me. First, since soucouyants remove their skin and then put it back on in the morning, their skin stretches and they appear wrinkled or their faces become lopsided. Christine demonstrated this by pulling her face out of shape. Second, soucouyants can fly only at night and must return to their human form during the day, so women who are soucouyants will not be about much during the day. They will be too tired from their activities of the previous night. Third, jealousy usually motivates them and so, in human form, they are prone to spreading malicious gossip. For example, a woman who spreads gossip that might lead to the break up of a couple might be a soucouyant. When I asked her if there was a similar thing for men, she said, "Sure Dee, that's the louga'ou!" The louga'ou is a man who turns into a kind of werewolf at night and attacks people on the road. Another pair of shape-changing creatures is the dyab and dyabess (devils).

Chapter 6 Folklore, Greetings, and Morality in Dominica

mous

Dangerous
Dyab
Dyabess

Immoral
Shape-Changers
Soucouyant
Louga'ou

Moral
comportment
Human

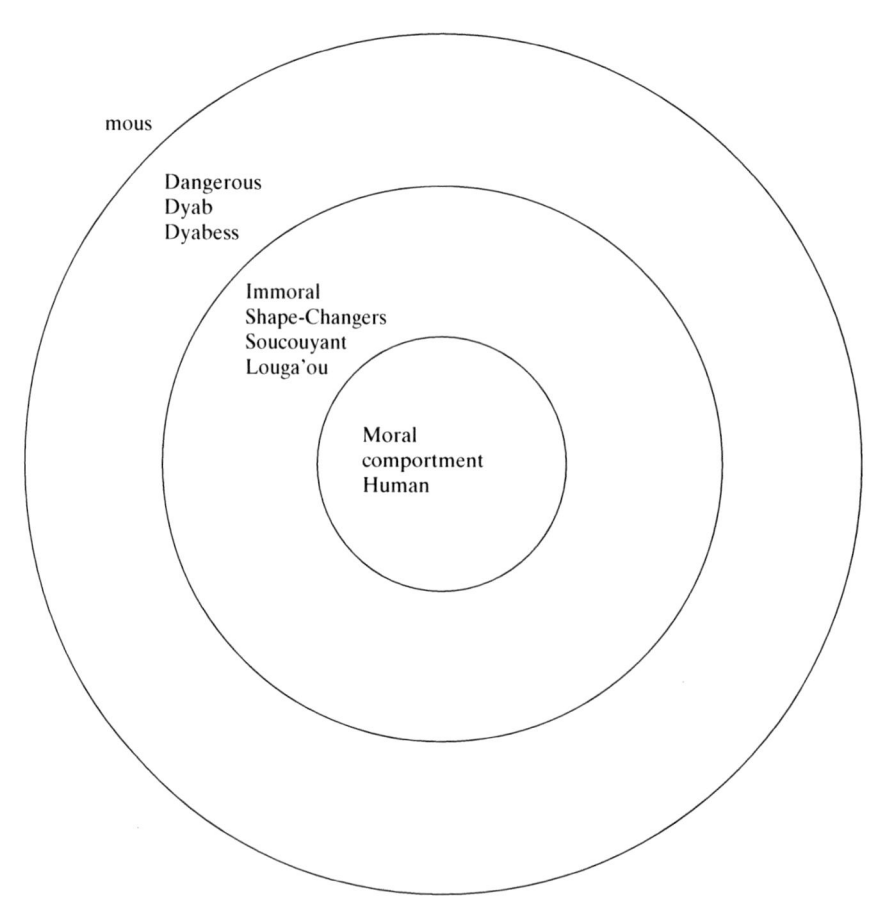

FIGURE 6.1

Map of the Moral Community.

If a person chooses to live alone, apart from any community, people will come to believe that the person is a dyab (if male) or dyabess (if female). These evil creatures take on human form to lure children to their deaths, usually by enticing them into a river.[iii] Recognition and respect for others and involvement in the community then are important indicators of a person's moral worth and indeed their very humanity. People refer to this as consciousness or "knowing how it is." The soucouyant and louga'ou are people who display antisocial traits (e.g., jealousy) and are rarely seen during the day. Still human, these beings change shape at night, becoming evil, destructive creatures that will eventually kill their victims. People who do not follow greeting protocols remain human, but people question their morality, including their sexual mores. Community membership and interaction are essential components of moral comportment in

Dominica. Failure to interact with and acknowledge others calls one's morality, and in more extreme violations, one's very humanity, into question.

CONSCIOUSNESS "WE MAY NOT HAVE MONEY, BUT WE HAVE FOOD."

> *... if work is to be the basis of true self-consciousness, it must derive from what I have termed above "consciousness of ability," something which is able to deal with the "universal might" [death]*
>
> ***Gadamer 1971: 71***

Many Dominicans limit their interactions with capitalism and the consumer marketplace. Most people grow some or most of their own food and build their own homes. Some Dominicans also make their own coal pots, fashion their own brooms, mattresses (stuffed with coconut fibre), and pillows (stuffed with feathers), and in true "roots Rasta"[iv] households, their own fabric, clothing, and shoes. Rastafarians explicitly refer to this practice as "consciousness."

As we saw in Chapter 3, during the period of slavery, slaves were "given" materials to build a chattel house and a plot of land where they were forced to produce most of their own provisions. They were, however, allowed to sell any surplus they could produce in the marketplace, and keep the proceeds. The earnings from these sales could go towards the purchase of freedom. Today, many people still associate economic self-sufficiency (vis-à-vis the cash economy) with freedom, likewise the ability to fabricate the necessities of life. There is also a widespread distrust of capitalism and consumerism. This distrust has been reinforced by the banana wars and the imposition of structural adjustment policies,[v] and stems back to Dominica's colonial history and the experience of slavery. Upon emancipation the newly freed people found land, built their chattel houses, and created gardens. The colonial records are full of accounts of British magistrates and planters lamenting the serious labour shortage in Dominica, referred to as the "ordeal of free labour" (Trouillot 1989: 704). The people, newly emancipated, were reluctant to work for their former masters in any long-term capacity, refusing for example to sign contracts. In his article on the naming of the peasantry in Dominica, Troulliot (1989: 704-5) notes that, while this phenomenon was not restricted to Dominica, "apprehensions about the independence of the newly freed population took more concrete forms in territories where land was particularly abundant." Dominica was one such territory. Economic self-sufficiency requires mutual cooperation and reciprocity. Greeting protocols enforce mutual recognition. With the increasing penetration of global capital into the Dominican economy, and increasing interaction with peoples from alienated consumerist over-developed economies come stories about how moral standards are eroding. These stories tell of "people not showing respect like they used to," and, in another phrase I heard many times during my visits to Dominica: "People not pulling together like they used to."

"PEOPLE NOT PULLING TOGETHER LIKE THEY USED TO."

In November 1997 a mountain in the interior collapsed, causing a massive landslide. Sand and debris inundated the Layou River, one of Dominica's longest, deepest, and most beautiful rivers, causing flooding and threatening the villages along the river, especially those near the Caribbean coast. Miraculously, there were no fatalities; however, some people lost land and crops to the flood. As would be the case anywhere, people tried to find explanations for the calamity, and these made up a good portion of conversation on busses and in village shops for several weeks following the disaster. Explanations fell into certain categories. First was the "scientific" explanation. Massive deforestation was the culprit, an unspecified "they" had been cutting down trees, the roots of the trees had been holding the sand (tarish) in place, the removal of this web led to the landslide. Given the overall ethos previously identified, this explanation seems to imply that (again) greed leads to destruction. Another popular explanation was that "the Americans" were testing a ground missile and had blown up the mountain, "You see what they do to their own, imagine what they could do to us." In another version, another foreign group whose development plans had gone awry when the government refused building permits had blown up the mountain in retaliation. These two explanations point to the deliberate, malign action of a foreign group motivated by greed, revenge, or lust for power. Another widespread set of explanations cited nature or God. In these accounts, God had sent the disaster to remind Dominicans of the need to work together. "People not pulling together like they used to." "Remember after David?"[vi] People really pulled together then." "They had to, wi."

A couple of days after Independence Day 1996 I saw pictures that depicted the idea of "pulling together" quite literally. Angela, a friend, was showing me photographs she took on Community Day of Service about ten years earlier. One of the photographs showed a group of men of all ages pulling a chattel house, secured by ropes, along the main road. In the past, co-operative labour exchange, the koudmen, would also occur during land-clearing and house construction (Berleant-Schiller and Maurer 1993: 72). Usually men would perform the manual labour and women would prepare the food, which they would serve along with portions of rum to the workers after they had completed their task. Community Day of Service represents an attempt to preserve a tradition, which, as Angela and others told me, was more common "before." The following year, Gerald, a friend in the north part of Dominica, moved his home in this fashion. His wife and a friend's sister prepared a broth and provided drinks for the workers. The difference was that for this move, they enlisted the help of a pick-up truck. The owner of the truck charged a cash fee for his services. Telling me about this, Gerald noted, "People not pulling together like they used to."

Self-reliance in this sense is not the isolated, alienated individual of modern industrial capitalist society. People related their anxieties about satellite television, grocery chains and increased use of packaged foods, tourism, mining, and deforestation in terms of decay in the moral fabric of society: people are not greeting one another, they are not pulling together like before. The hybridization of culture is not about black and white like the racist theories of colonial era, it is about radically different systems of values—how to metre social change without destroying the moral fibre of Dominican society. All of this is intimately, and in complex ways, connected with attitudes towards sexuality, particularly female sexuality.

POLITICAL ECONOMY, FEMALE GENDER ROLES, AND SEXUALITY

> *... Dominicans say, as do people everywhere in the Caribbean, "This Island is one big family you know!" This conceptualisation of community as family alerts us immediately to the problems of applying a domestic/public opposition in the region.*
>
> ***Berleant-Schiller and Maurer 1993: 68***

In their article on feminist theory and women's networks in Barbuda and Dominica, Riva Berleant-Schiller and William M. Maurer (1993) have argued that "the western assumption that social life is divided into two spheres, the public, usually dominated by men, and the domestic, usually dominated by women" cannot be assumed to apply cross-culturally (1993: 65). In the Caribbean, they state, this "distinction holds up best when we are talking about men's roles" but the two domains become less distinct in relation to women's roles (ibid). Berleant-Schiller and Maurer "explore the ways in which the public and domestic domains merge in women's roles in two islands of the Lesser Antilles, Dominica and Barbuda." To do this they focus on "intra island economy and informal social organisation." They demonstrate that women's roles "are integral to a range of social and economic processes" that are not restricted to the household (Berleant-Schiller and Maurer 1993: 65). Women's continuous contribution to economic and community life in the Caribbean has been described as "perhaps outstanding" by Judith Gussler.

Writing about St. Kitts, Gussler argues that where resources are scarce cooperation becomes essential. "[T]he social system itself depends on the ability of the female to be mobile, flexible and resourceful rather than tied to a specific structure or role (Gussler 1980: 208; Berleant-Schiller and Maurer 1993: 66). Berleant-Schiller and Maurer identify "general types" of social roles and activities that link private and public including "networking, marketing and religious activities" (1993: 66). In Dominica, women are the majority of sellers in the markets in Roseau and Portsmouth. Women own and manage the majority of rum shops and snack stalls, and operate many of the refreshment stands at cultural events. Even those activities that directly relate to household maintenance such as washing clothes and washing dishes are often public events in Dominica. Many women still wash their clothes and dishes in the many crystal-clear rivers around the island. In areas with access to tap water, women wash in large plastic tubs in the yard, which they usually share with other women. Even the newer launderettes are sites for meeting and exchanging news and gossip. The marketplace, shops, and church steps are other hubs for the news that keeps social networks in place, and again women dominate these locales.

REPUTATION, RESPECTABILITY, AND DOMINICA'S MORAL COMMUNITY

Peter Wilson's *Crab Antics*, first published in 1971, proposed new way of looking at society and culture in the Caribbean. Wilson's ethnography, based on his fieldwork in the island he called Providencia, attempted to understand the totality of social life in Providencia, and by extension, to propose a model applicable to all societies in the region. The value orientation shared by the inhabitants of Provedencia was rooted in a sense of place:

> *... social life in general arises out of the continuing relations of people to each other in space and time and with space and time. In the first instance, men in their relations must adapt to the environment; in the second instance they appropriate it. Thus the people living permanently in a particular place and nowhere else (e.g. Providencia) at a given time (i.e. now) share this placement and contemporaneity as the lower common denominator of their specific and shared identity. In this broad sense of space and time they can consider each other as equals. To a great extent, in their perception of their relationship to a fixed and autonomous environment and in their differentiation from those attached to another environment, people are each others' moral equals. In turn, this common environment, as experience, is called upon to justify this claim to equality.*
> Wilson 1971: 8

This section has analyzed and described Dominica's moral landscape, or value orientation, to provide a foundation for understanding people's anxieties about the effects of the processes of globalization.

Respectability relates to the degree of appropriation of the environment, and the stratification that results from "what people *think* to be significant as difference" (Wilson 1971: 8). Reputation rests on a principle of egalitarianism. "There is, however, a particular level of [social] structure which is the dialectical complement of respectability and which supports an ideal of sociological equality." (Wilson, 1971: 9)

The structure of Caribbean social life is, then, the dialectical relation between the two principles, respectability and reputation. This is what is being expressed by the more observable features of social relations and social behaviour; but in the end I would argue that all levels of the structure are explicable as products of reputation, respectability, and the dialectical relation between them. On Providencia this relationship is known as the crab antics, *hence the title of this book.*

Wilson 1971: 9

Wilson argued that reputation was "largely specific to men," and respectability "particular to women" and to men only at certain times in their lives (Wilson 1971: 9). Respectability, he further argued, "has its roots in the external colonizing (or quasi-colonizing) society" and reputation is "indigenous" to the colony.

In Dominica, reputation and respectability form one moral system or value orientation that encompasses the lives of men and women, and cuts across class lines. It is not based on a binary distinction between an African or indigenous value system and a British or European system but rather is the product of a set of processes set in motion during the colonial era that combined elements of the various moralities that the people who first peopled the colony carried with them. Historically, it is the result of negotiations that emerged through the historical interactions among Carib; French; British; Italian; Spanish; Ibo, Yoruba, and other West African tribes; and slaves transported from other islands in the Caribbean. The majority were forged on the plantations with the daily interaction between European planters and overseers and African slaves (see Chapter 3). The processes continue in the present time, and the forms and conditions of these contemporary interactions are the subject of the next chapter.

CHAPTER **SUMMARY**

Key Terms

CONSCIOUSNESS – Here used in the "emic" sense, a term used by Dominicans to refer to a certain value orientation that includes an emphasis on mutual recognition and on making rather than buying things.

LOUGA'OU – Something like a werewolf, one of the shape-changers that features in Dominican folklore, always a man.

MASTER/SLAVE DIALECTIC - A series of passages from Hegel's *Phenomenology of Spirit*, taken up by Caribbean and African scholars in the diaspora to argue for a different kind of awareness shaped by the historical experience of slavery.

MORAL COMPORTMENT - Ideas about the way a person should carry themselves in public—how to walk, how to dress, whether or not one should greet people or make eye contact, etc. This will vary from culture to culture.

MOUS - A genie or demon that people create when they want wealth and power over others. Dangerous as a mous will usually "turn" making itself the master and its maker the slave.

REPUTATION AND RESPECTABILITY - A theoretical framework, proposed by anthropologist Peter Wilson, as a way of looking at Caribbean societies, especially gender relations.

SOUCOUYANT - A shape-changer, always a woman when in human form, who flies around at night and sucks the blood of her human victims.

Discussion Questions

1. What was "the problem of free labour"?

2. Do you agree with the author's interpretation of the story of the mous? Why/Why not?

3. Do the greeting protocols relate in any way to the forms of dance or music described earlier in this ethnography?

4. How do ideas about the soucouyants, louga'ou, and persons believed to have made mous relate to the tradition of chante mas and calypso described in Chapter 5?

5. What is the framework of "reputation and respectability"?

NOTES

[i] I provide a slightly more nuanced interpretation of this in another paper (Rose, 2009).

[ii] I heard this story on three separate occasions, in three different villages. Each time I was shown a home and told to avoid the descendents of this witch.

[iii] Gary Smith, personal communication.

[iv] Dominicans distinguish between different modes of Rastafarianism, some of which refer to beliefs (Selassie Rastas, for example) and some of which refer to lifestyle or practice. Roots Rastas are most in tune with nature, tend to live in "Zion" (in the mountains), and tend to have the least interaction with Babylon (town, cash, commodities, and technology).

PART 3
GLOBALIZATION: CONTACT AND CULTURAL CHANGE

7
CONTINUITY AND CHANGE: CREOLIZATION AND GLOBALIZATION TODAY

In this short monograph I have focused on aspects of Dominican national and village level self-representations of their own aesthetic traditions. My intention has been to demonstrate how these traditions are celebrated by Dominicans, on the ground, in performances put on by and for themselves. In particular, Chapter 4 described the creole culture that is celebrated by Dominicans during their Heritage Day and Independence Day activities. Chapter 5 described calypso and other cultural forms related to Carnival, including a performance depicting a version of Dominican history as forged by the interaction of diverse peoples and the resulting sense of a national identity encompassed by the term "bouyon." Historically, these cultural forms and value orientations emerged through the interaction of Indigenous, West-African, and various European cultures over three centuries on the island of Dominica (and throughout the Caribbean region). Both the emergence and celebration of creolization and the political and economic circumstances under which the languages, modes of dress, and dance described in the preceding chapters emerged demonstrate that the processes encompassed by the term "globalization" are not new for the Caribbean region (Mintz 1977).

Movement of peoples, hybridization, and flows of transnational capital and commodities have been characteristics of the Caribbean region for several centuries. Recent decades have seen a continuation of these aspects of life in the region, albeit in new forms. While the previous chapters focused mainly on Creole *traditions* rooted in the past and celebrated during various festivals throughout the year as part of a national Dominican identity, this chapter will look at some recent changes in the perception of Creole identity in Dominica and globally. The shift here is to an examination of the interaction between local and global forces that are taking place *both* internationally *and* on the island itself. For example, international neo-liberal economic policies have been imposed on Dominica by external forces, as have certain ideas about the island and the region through international mass media. How do the government and people of Dominica adopt, adapt, and reinvent under present-day conditions? Specifically, we will look at the Dominica World Creole Music Festival, the filming of the Disney series *Pirates of the Caribbean,* and the construction of the Model Carib Village (*Kalinago Barana Autê*). Each of these new additions to Dominica's cultural landscape relate, in different ways, to global and local understandings about identities, borders, the melding of cultural forms. Each provides an example of the ways that the Dominican government and population are attempting to find solutions to their economic problems and the ways in which they are able or unable to negotiate between their own self-representations and those of the international mass media. In other words, the continued interplay between "local" or Dominican culture and livelihood and "global" or international representations and desires will be the focus of this chapter. First we will look at changes to Dominica's economy and the resulting increase in the country's reliance on tourism as a major impetus driving recent cross-cultural interactions there.

CHANGES IN DOMINICA'S ECONOMY
THE CRISIS IN DOMINICA'S BANANA INDUSTRY

In the Caribbean,

> *The development of the capitalist economy on a world scale has been crucial in shaping the micro-structure and systems of the rural economy. All important systemic relations—what land is used and by whom; what is produced and with what technology; how it is marketed; who consumes it; and in what form—have been governed by what must have appeared for most of the region's history to be inexorable laws of an expanding world economy.*
>
> *Thomas 1996: 243–244*

Since its "discovery" in 1492 the Caribbean has been a site of economic production and consumption, subject to the control of European centres of power, and Dominica, as we have seen, is no exception to this. For centuries the production of agricultural crops from coffee and sugar during the Plantation Era, to limes and then bananas in more recent times, Dominican agricultural workers, from slaves to independent peasants, have been producing for local consumption and for export. Changes in international trade agreements beginning in the mid-1990s have transformed the economies of many of the island nations of the Caribbean from agricultural production to spaces of consumption and leisure (Patullo 2005; Smith 2006). These changes have led to the virtual destruction of the banana industry in Dominica, forcing the government to turn to tourism as a "last resort" for economic survival. Tourism, it is hoped, will offer a source of employment for Dominica's citizens and provide stability for the country's economy.

On June 23, 2000 an agreement between the European Community and its member states and members of the African, Caribbean and Pacific (ACP) group of states was signed in Cotonou, Benin. This agreement, known as the "Cotonou Agreement," will expire in 2020. The agreement temporarily extends the protection formerly afforded to ACP banana producers under Lomé IV.[i] However, most banana farmers in Dominica have little confidence in their economic future as is evidenced by the sharp and steady decline in banana production there. The Cotonou Agreement marked the final chapter in an ongoing trade dispute dubbed the "Banana Wars" by the news media. The "eight year standoff between the European Union and the USA over bananas" had dire consequences, especially for smaller Caribbean nations such as Dominica, St. Lucia, St. Vincent, and the Grenadines. (Myers 2004: 1) From the time of my first arrival in Dominica, anxieties surrounding this trade dispute were a frequent topic of conversation and for good reason.

In 1994, agriculture remained a significant contributor to Gross Domestic Product (GDP), but was already showing a decline from the 1980s. Between 1988 and 1999 the banana industry of Dominica recorded a 63 percent decline in production and a 62 percent decline in export value. There was also a corresponding decline in the number of farmers and acreage under bananas. Many farmers have abandoned their fields, especially those dependent on labour. By 2004, agriculture dropped to 17.7 percent of Dominica's GDP while services accounted for nearly 50 percent. However, agriculture continued to employ a large segment of the working population (40 percent). The unemployment rate was nearly 25 percent by 2000 and the population living below the poverty line was at 30 percent (CIA 1994). At the national level, Dominica has now moved from a position of net exporter of agri-food products to net importer (see Table 7.1), and it is very likely that this situation will continue because of the openness of the economy and the changing food habits of the population (Campbell 2001).

Thus, the decline in banana production marks a significant change for Dominicans. For most of its recorded history, Dominica has been the provider of agricultural crops for metropole countries. Dominican farmers have also been growing the bulk of their own subsistence crops. Since Emancipation, much of this farming has taken place on independent peasant farms and a culture based on relative independence from the cash economy, self-sufficiency, and an ethos of respect and caring has emerged (see Chapter 6). The crisis in the banana industry, therefore, marks more than an economic disaster—it also has social and cultural implications. In the economic realm, there have been four results:

1. Increased emigration
2. Alienation of land from the agricultural sector
3. Increased reliance on imported goods
4. Increased reliance on the tourism sector

Table 7.1   Trade Balance 1991–1995, Campbell 2001

AGRICULTURAL TRADE	1991	1992	1993	1994	1995
Imports	76.6	76.6	68.9	72.7	82.8
Exports	96.5	96.5	84.8	70.0	60.9
Trade Balance	19.9	19.9	14.1	−2.7	−21.9

Both the increase in emigration and the increased reliance on tourism for economic stability and development have led to changes in Dominican policies, including the decision to add "cultural tourism" to the previous initiative promoting Dominica as the "Nature Island." With this shift has come a need to entice visitors to come to the island. Dominica, given its infrastructure and wild terrain, has had to carve a niche based on three features: its status as the "Nature Island of the Caribbean"; its creole culture; and the relatively large Kalinago (Carib) population. In the following sections, we will look at the effects of the tourist interaction and tourist promotions on creole and indigenous culture in Dominica by looking at the World Creole Music Festival, the filming of the *Pirates of the Caribbean* and the construction of the *Kalinago Barana Autê* or Model Carib Village. Each of these, in part, marks the efforts of the government to alleviate the negative economic and social impacts of the crisis in the banana industry by developing the country's tourist sector.

TOURISM

As we have seen, the formation of the European Economic Union and the regulations devised by the General Agreement on Tariff and Trade, enforced by the World Trade Organization, have affected banana producers in African, Caribbean, and Pacific nations. As a country whose economy was heavily invested in small-scale production of bananas for export to the United Kingdom, Dominica's economy was among those hardest hit by these events. Three of the direct results of this economic crisis have already been addressed: emigration; the abandoning of agricultural lands as small-holders abandon their farms in search of employment elsewhere; and an increased reliance on imported commodities. A related effect of this crisis has been a steady increase in tourist visits, as successive Dominican governments have come to view tourism as the "last resort" for economic survival (Patullo 2005). Emigration, immigration, and tourism are not new to Dominica; however, what is new is the volume of arrivals (See Figure 7.1) and the perceived lack of any viable alternative. The remainder of this chapter will examine the creative ways that the government and people of Dominica have tried to adapt to the changed circumstances of their conditions for making a livelihood. These solutions have been forged in relation to images of the region and the island in the mass media.

IMAGES OF THE CARIBBEAN: PARADISE, PLAYGROUND, AND PIRATES

Web-sites promoting tourism in the Caribbean Region usually depict the islands as virtually uninhabited and undeveloped. Images of lush, tropical rainforests; pristine waterfalls; and wild oceans with crashing waves, often with no people in the photographs, present the image of a pristine, untouched paradise. Another set of images focuses on hotels, swimming pools, beaches, casinos, restaurants, and water sports. If people are included, they are almost always tourists, usually white and usually depicted in couples or foursomes (all heterosexual in the ads I saw) and are depicted swimming, waterskiing, or in some sort of romantic pose—a romantic or fun playground. Dominica, with its rugged terrain, has not used these images to promote visitors to the island, but has instead focused on its image as the "Nature Island" of the Caribbean, emphasizing its position as a tropical paradise to promote eco-tourism.

TROPICAL PARADISE

> *You can be a part of the wildlife while you're in Dominica, playing hide and seek among endless tropical rainforests, enjoying romantic interludes in emerald pools and under waterfalls . . .*
> *Ott 2002*

> *The relatively few visitors who make their way to Dominica find an extraordinary place, a bit of the Caribbean that retains its pristine nature. . . .*
> *Wissing, 1999*

These articles, written by North American travel writers, encourage people to "frolic with nature" and enjoy "romantic interludes" in public places. Yet people can easily be unaware of the fact that Dominica's rivers and waterfalls are, in fact, public places; not appropriate for "romantic interludes." The idea of a wild, untouched land, reminiscent of *terra nullis,* ignores the fact that Dominica has been inhabited by human beings, with their respective technologies and economic activities, for thousands of years. The images further suggest that this "pristine wilderness" should be preserved for the benefit of tourists from developed countries in their nostalgic longing for those aspects of nature long ago destroyed or marginalized by capitalist development. Renato Rosaldo (1989) calls this "Imperial Nostalgia," which he defines as regret and desire for all that has been destroyed through colonialism or industrialization.

A TROPICAL PLAYGROUND

In recent years, cruise ship arrivals accounted for the majority of visitors and represented the fastest growing tourist sector in Dominica. A different set of marketing images targets most of these travelers. A brief look at some of these images may help us to understand the behavior of the four cruise ship passengers who neglected to respond to Josephine's greeting or even acknowledge her presence (see Chapter 6).

A survey of more than fifty web-sites advertising hotels and destinations throughout the Caribbean, including many web-sites specifically promoting

Cruise Ship Arrivals 1991–2004

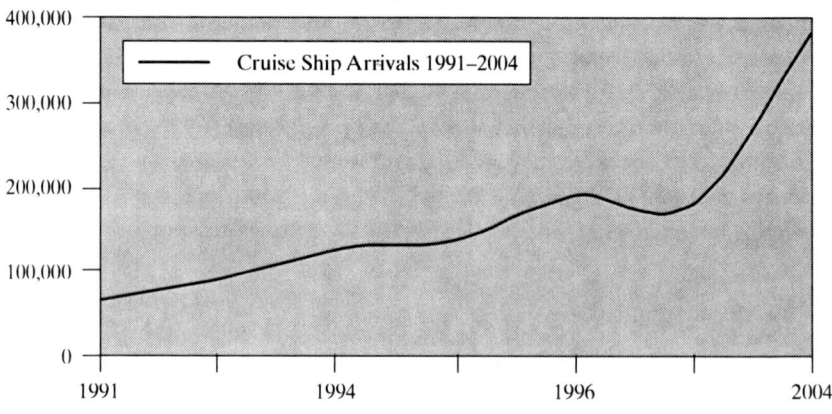

FIGURE 7.1

Cruise Ship Passenger[ii] Arrivals to Dominica 1991–2004
Sources: Adapted from "Arrivals by Cruise ship January–December 1990–1996 *Commonwealth of Dominica Central Statistics Office Travel Report for 1996* and Caribbean Press Releases.com

cruises, revealed a clear pattern. The images featured white sand beaches, tropical flora and fauna, waterfalls, hot springs, colonial sites, and on-board sleeping, dining, and entertainment facilities. Of the few images that included people, the majority depicted tourists, usually white, enjoying the amenities. Romance was a major theme. A long-playing television commercial boasted that there was no need for aphrodisiacs in the Caribbean. Most of the on-line images depicted a couple, usually posed embracing or gazing into one another's eyes. The couples were usually alone whether they were posed on the beach, under or by a waterfall, in hot springs, or in their rooms. Images featuring groups of tourists focused on "fun" activities such as water sports. People who were clearly "locals" were conspicuously absent from most of the images. When "locals" did appear in advertisements, they were smiling and usually serving or entertaining their guests.

In all these ads, the message is, rather blatantly, that the Caribbean exists for the pleasure, convenience, and comfort of the tourists. Members of the host population, if present at all, are there to serve and entertain. One site offered a "Bahama Mama" cruise, another offered tourists their own "Vacation Nanny." Dominica has in fact avoided using these types of images to promote their tourist package, instead using adventure, culture, and their indigenous population as features unique to the island. The World Creole Music Festival was one of the first major initiatives to this end.

THE WORLD CREOLE MUSIC FESTIVAL

In 1997 the Dominica Festivals Commission inaugurated the first World Creole Music Festival. According to the official web-site, "This festival is widely seen as one of the only truly indigenous music event in Dominica and the Eastern Caribbean by extension." The impetus for the festival was to "provide a platform for Dominican musicians and musical expressions, and to increase the island's visibility overseas." The organizers also hoped that the introduction of the new, international festival would boost tourism and "promote creole music as a major musical art form." The festival takes place annually, on the last weekend of October, thus ensuring that it overlaps with Dominica's Independence Day festivities, without actually interfering with them. In its first year, it attracted 10 000 visitors, by 2007 that number had reached 25 000. Musicians playing cadence lypso, soca, zouk, reggae, and zydeco have played at the festival and represent creole musical forms from Africa, North America, various French islands of the Caribbean and of course Dominica. According to the festival's official web-site which is used to promote the festival to an international audience, the festival has provided a platform for musical genres that "have their roots in various forms of musical fusion from the countries of the creole-speaking world." (http://www.wcf.dom)

I had the good fortune to be able to attend the festival in 1997 and again in 1999. The festival did indeed attract visitors to the island and provide a venue for Dominican musicians, including some who now live in other countries. But it also provided a place for Dominicans to celebrate newer forms of music and a space to situate themselves as both a part of a wider, regional art form and as distinctly Dominican. The festival took place at Festival City in Roseau and the grounds were full of revellers, some from overseas, many from Dominica. The perimeter of the gated outdoor arena was lined with stalls selling food and beverages, including beer and soft drinks, pizza, and conch water. Outside of the arena, additional vendors had set up their own stalls featuring barbequed chicken and fish, beer, and soft drinks. Refreshments provided outside the gates were less expensive, but meant missing some of the action. The atmosphere was like Carnival, although not quite as participatory. People danced and moved to the various rhythms and were especially excited by the appearance of Congolese performer Sakis. Dominican artists, including WCK and reggae singer Nasio Fontaine to name just two, also received a warm reception. The World Creole Music Festival brought the world to Dominica, at least the creole-speaking world, and put Dominica on the world stage. The idea for the festival and its content were designed and in the control of Dominican officials and festival organizers. However, images of Dominica and the region are also generated by external forces besides tourist promotions. Another event that hurled Dominica into the global imagination was the filming of the blockbuster trilogy *Pirates of the Caribbean*.

PIRATES

A recent addition to the images of the region, and of Dominica in particular, can be found in the Disney trilogy *Pirates of the Caribbean,* starring Johnny Depp as pirate Jack Sparrow.[iii] The second and third installments of this series were filmed on location in Dominica and neighboring islands. A press release issued by the government explained that Dominica was an "ideal filming location" for the film because of its "natural heritage, unspoiled scenic beauty" and its peoples and culture and pointed out that Dominica is also "home to the last remaining settlement of Indigenous Peoples of the Caribbean."(Caribbean Press Release.com 2006).

Material included in the official press release demonstrates the ways that Dominica is represented as a desirable location and uses Disney's choice of their island as a way to also attract tourists; indeed, most of the finanacial gain to the population came not from jobs generated by the filming, since Disney brought most of their crew from the United States, but in increased tourist visits by the many fans of the film. However, the filming of the movie did bring some employment to Dominicans. Most of the jobs given to Dominicans were restricted to service type jobs—cooking and cleaning for the film crew, and the occasional part as an extra, for example. One man who was hired to harvest coconuts lest one "fall on a Hollywood head" earned enough money to build a small house. (Patullo 2006) While the few jobs provided were welcome in a country struggling with high unemployment rates and the decline in the agricultural sector described above, the filming came at a cost. Dominica's Kalinago population, although divided on the issue, tended to object to the film's portrayal of a cannibalistic indigenous group. Chief Charles Williams, the Carib Chief at the time, made a public, global appeal objecting to the filming of the second installment on the island. He closed his objection with an appeal to:

> *condemn that act of victimization and stigmatization by all those who promote and support it, money is not always the answer . . .*
>
> *I thank you.*
> *Chief Charles Williams*

These closing words of Chief Williams' objection point to a conflict in value orientations—between those values outlined in Chapter 6 and those of an individualistic and materialistic nature. Chief Williams' main objection was to film scenes portraying indigenous peoples of the region as cannibals in the second installment, *Dead Man's Chest*. The Disney Corporation constructed a "Cannibal Village," featuring cages made of human bones, and hired Dominican Carib people to work as extras portraying the cannibalistic people that had captured Sparrow and his crew. Although local Carib leaders had protested, the film was made according to script. "The representation of cannibals in the film takes the form of an absurd spoof of the most degrading cinematic representation of primitive tribes, adorned with bones, grease paint, a gruff language, and failing stone age technologies" (Sheller 2007: 29). It was not only the Carib people of Dominica who had reason to protest.

The film also portrayed an Afro-Caribbean obeah woman, or sorceress, and a voodoo-like ritual filmed in the Indian River in Dominica's north. Her lodgings were equipped with skulls and candles and charms and she had the ability to raise the dead. Finally, the movie portrayed stunning images of a wild, untamed frontier with lush verdant rainforest and steep, dangerous mountains. These images resonate with Dominican promotions attracting tourists to an "untouched eco-paradise for nature lovers" (Sheller 2007) described above. The movie thus echoed images found in tourism advertising for the region and for Dominica, but also evoked a wild frontier adventure and the presence of an indigenous population. In response to the demand created by these movies, Dominican hoteliers and tour guides have added several adventure packages, all drawing on the popularity of the movie, including tours that let you "walk in the steps of the stars" or enjoy a "special barbeque" in a reconstruction of the Cannibal Village depicted in the second installment of the trilogy. Another cultural tourism attraction that was built before, and without the negative stereotypes found in, the movie is the Kalinago Barana Auté or the Model Carib Village.

THE MODEL CARIB VILLAGE

The Carib Model Village (the Kalinago Barana Auté) is located near the Isukulati Falls along the banks of the Crayfish River in the Carib Territory (northeast section of the island). The village is the result of the 1994 Upgrading of Ecotourism Sites Project (UESP), an initiative of the Caribbean Development Bank. The work for the project began in 1998 and included the construction of an access road to enable tourists to reach the destination. The village offers cultural performances, canoe building workshops, cassava processing, and basket weaving as well as a gift shop and refreshment stand. Tourists cross a footbridge over the river and then follow a winding trail through the village populated by "Carib inspired" huts (Kalinago Barana Auté website). While the site promises a unique "historical" experience and offers features of Carib tradition that are still practiced, it is nonetheless also physically and culturally removed from the present-day reality of the lives of most Kalinago on the island.

In Dominica the presentation of a Carib cultural identity by the territories' two cultural groups, the Karifuna and the Karina, takes place through the production and sale of Carib baskets and weavings and through individually run cassava and canoe building workshops (Smith 2006: 72). All of these activities, however, take place in the Carib Territory, the area of the country where Carib people live, plant their fields, and work. The Carib Model Village is located outside of this area and this has caused it to be contentious. A major problem is that the model village was built to accommodate tourist needs and to enable a "one-stop" Carib experience that would not prevent tourists from visiting other parts of the island on the same day (recall that most tourist visits are made by people on a cruise who are able to select from a menu of one-day tours). On the other hand,

> *For communities who wish to express particular ideas of their past, the heritage center or cultural museum, whilst remaining an economic transaction, has also contained the hope of communicating local understandings of history and identity.*
>
> *Smith 2006: 72*

The development of the Model Carib Village then provides a spatial location for a condensed representation of Kalinago indigenous identity and a potential source of revenue for Kalinago men and women. However, since the site is removed from the daily lives of these same men and women, and part of what is found in this village belongs to the past, for example the grass huts, not everybody is in agreement as to its real benefits. Thus, as with the packages inspired by the *Pirates of the Caribbean*, it represents part of a global conversation where the interaction between representations and reality are creating blurred boundaries, reproducing stereotypes, but also opening spaces for the assertion of a local identity. As with the creole cultural forms from previous eras, tourism seems to involve the creative play between resistance and accommodation, adopting and adapting for survival.

FUTURE RESEARCH DIRECTIONS

> *Along the entire creolising spectrum, from First World metropolis to Third World village, through education and popular culture, by way of missionaries, consultants, critical intellectuals, and small town storytellers, a conversation between cultures goes on.*
>
> **Hannerz 1987: 555**

Given its early association with colonialism and slavery, some scholars question the applicability of the concept of creolization in our understandings of present-day changes elsewhere, calling for attention to the historical specificity of creolization in the Caribbean (Mintz and Price 1992; Sheller 2002). For others, such as Ulf Hannerz, creolization is a theoretical concept that provides anthropologists with tools to pursue broader questions regarding cultural change and social transformations that take place through sustained interactions between people from different ethnic groups. As such, creolization is seen as a useful concept for understanding transformations occurring through the intense movement of peoples and images under the current conditions connected to globalization. The question now will be what sorts of transformations will occur in creole expressive culture as it becomes a part of a global tourism product? International attention brings a sense of pride and unites Dominican creole artists, especially musicians, with other creole artists. Such events foster the creation of a strong, transnational creole identity.

Cultural sites like the Model Carib Village enable a platform for the presentation of an indigenous identity. Potential problems arise, however, when the representations of a region are generated by external sources with their own histories and fantasies and desires. As we saw with the *Pirates of the Caribbean* trilogy, stereotyped images may rule the day. The ways that the people of Dominica responded to the conflicting images—some of which complemented their own tourism package and some of which did not, demonstrate resourcefulness but also highlight some of the dangers of cultural tourism.

The historical record and celebration of creole traditions in Dominica suggest that ". . . elaborations of these processes have contributed to our more general understanding of how the maintenance of an alternative and potentially oppositional worldview is often simultaneous to the adoption, adaptation, and modification of previously "foreign" cultural forms and practices" (Slocum and Thomas 2003: 556). The ways that the tourist sector and individual Dominicans have adopted and adapted those images imposed upon them by international mass media through tourism advertisements, travel writing, and a fantasy movie suggest that the creative resistance of their forebears is still alive and well. The future challenge, it seems, will be to maintain control over the representations of the island and the nature of tourist interactions there. Initiatives such as the World Creole Music Festival afford an opportunity to showcase Dominican musical innovations and provide a platform for Dominican musicians while also generating tourist revenue for the island. It seems appropriate that as part of that festival, Dominica's WCK band performs their bouyon music for the world.

Creole cultures and more recent changes brought about by globalization today need always be understood in terms of their own historical circumstances. In this monograph, I have privileged the view of Dominicans. It remains to be seen how well they will be able to maintain control over their culture, however, the iniatives described in this chapter suggest that there is a great deal of cultural awareness and pride in both traditions and innovations that should serve the country well in these trying times.

CHAPTER **SUMMARY**

Key Terms

BANANA WARS - the phrase used to refer to the trade dispute between the United States and European Union and the African, Caribbean, and Pacific nations whose banana export industry was protected by the Lomé protocol.

CULTURAL TOURISM - used to describe a type of tourism where the visitors select a destination based on their interest in some aspect or aspects of the host country's cultural traditions or history.

ECO-TOURISM - used to describe a type of tourism where the visitors select a destination based on their interest in some aspect or aspects of the natural setting including flora and fauna, or geographical features such as waterfalls or rainforest.

IMPERIAL NOSTALGIA - a phrase used to describe a motivating force behind cultural and eco-tourism. Coined by Renato Rosaldo, the phrase highlights nostalgia for things destroyed by industrialization and colonialism.

Discussion Questions

1. What might be some of the effects on Dominican culture that arise as a result of the increased dependence on tourism?

2. Compare and contrast the World Creole Music Festival and the Model Carib Village.

3. What effects have global neo-liberal economic policies and changes in international trade agreements had on the island of Dominica?

4. Do you think that the concept of creolization should be used only to analyze changes under particular circumstances or do you agree with Ulf Hannerz that the concept has wider applicability? Why/Why not?

5. Why did Chief Charles Williams object to the portrayal of cannibals in the Disney movie *Pirates of the Caribbean*? Do you agree with his objections? Why/Why not?

FURTHER READING

A Forte, Maximillian (ed.) 2006.

Indigenous Resurgence in the Contemporary Caribbean - Amerindian Survival and Revival. New York: Peter Lang Publishing Inc.

Jayawardena, Chandana (ed.) 2002.
> *Tourism and Hospitality Education and Training in the Caribbean.* Kingston, Jamaica: University of West Indies Press.

Myers, Gordon 2004.
> *The Banana Wars – The Price of Free Trade.* London: Zed Books.

Patullo, Polly 2005.
> *Last Resorts; The Cost of Tourism in the Caribbean.* New York: New York University Press.

VIDEOS/DVDS

Black, Stephanie (Producer and Director) 2001. *Life and Debt.*

WEB - LINKS

Banana Wars—Caribbean
> http://www.youtube.com/watch?v=1KLXpm9nrT0

Dominica World Creole Music Festival
> http://www.wcmfdominica.com

Kalinago Barana Autê web-site
> http://www.kalinagobaranaaute.com/

NOTES

[i] This is the name of the trade agreement that offered special, duty-free access for ACP bananas being imported into their former colonial metropole country. In the case of Dominica and other islands that had been subject to British rule, this access was to the United Kingdom. See further reading section and web-links for more information on the "banana wars."

[ii] Cruise ship arrivals includes Windjammers. Windjammers are not regular cruise lines, but are smaller yachts that arrive on a regular basis.

[iii] Of course, the association of privateers or pirates with the Caribbean region has historical precedent.

Anderson, Benedict 1991.

Imagined Communities – Reflections on the Origin and Spread of Nationalism. London and New York: Verso.

Atwood, Thomas 1791.

The History of the Island of Dominica. London: J. Johnson.

Baker, Patrick 1994.

Centring the periphery : chaos, order, and the ethnohistory of Dominica. Montreal: McGill – Queens University Press.

Baromé, Joseph 1972.

Spain and Dominica 1493–1647, The French and Dominica 1699–1793, Dominica during French Occupation 1778–1784. In E. O. LeBlanc (ed), *Aspects of Dominican History.* Roseau, Dominica: Government Printing Division, pp. 67–103.

Beckles, Hilary McD 1999.

Centering Woman: Gender Discourses in Caribbean Slave Society. Kingston: Ian Randle, Publishers.

Berleant-Schiller, Riva and Bill Maurer 1993.

Women's Place is Every Place: Merging Domains and Women's Roles in Dominica and Barbuda. In Janet Momsen (ed.), *Women and Change in the Caribbean.* London: John Currey; Bloomington: Indiana University Press; Kingston, Jamaica: Ian Randle, pp. 65–79.

Bhabha, Homi 1994.

The Location of Culture. New York: Routledge.

Bernabe, Jean, Patrick Chamoiseau, Raphael Confiant, and Mohamed B. Taleb Kyher. 1990.

In Praise of Creoleness. *Callaloo* 13(4): 886–909.

Brathwaite, Edward Kamau 1974.

Contradictory Omens: Cultural Diversity and Integration in the Caribbean. Mona, Jamaica: Savacou.

Campbell, Dunstan 2001.

> Positioning Dominica's Agriculture for Sustained Economic and Social Development. http://www.uwichill.edu.bb/bnccde/dominica/conference/papers/CampbellD.html. Accessed March 7, 2003.

CarribeanPressRelease.com.

> http://www.caribbeanpressreleases.com/articles/79/1/Dominica-Announces-quotPirates-of-the-Caribbean-Packages/Hoteliers-Create-Special-Offers-in-Response-to-Interest-Created-by-Hit-Movie.html. Accessed October 18, 2008.
> http://www.caribbeanpressreleases.com/articles/7/1/Massive-Exposure-for-Dominica-with-Pirates-of-the-Caribbean-2/Exposure-for-Dominica-with-Pirates-of-the-Caribbean-Dead-Mans-Chest.html. Accessed October 18, 2008.

CIA 2008.

> The World Factbook, Dominica. https://www.cia.gov/library/publications/the-world-factbook/geos/do.html. Accessed October 18, 2008.

CIA 1994.

> http://www.umsl.edu/services/govdocs/wofact94/index.html. Accessed October 18, 2008.

Connel, John and Chris Gibson 2004.

> World Music: Deterritorializing Place and Identity. *Progress in Human Geography* 28(3): 342–361.

Cyrille, Dominique 2005.

> *Sa Ki Ta Nou* (This Belongs to Us) Creole Dances of the French Caribbean. In Susanna Sloat (ed.), *Caribbean Dance from* Abakua *to* Zouk*: How Movement Shapes Identity*. Florida: University Press of Florida, pp. 221–244.

D'Emilio, John and Estelle B. Freedman 1997.

> *Intimate Matters: A History of Sexuality in America*. 2nd edition. Chicago: University of Chicago Press.

Delphis Website, Dominica.

> http://www.delphis.dm/. Accessed February 12, 2005.

Dominica World Creole Music Festival Official Web-site.

> http://www.wcmfdominica.com. Accessed October 16, 2008.

List of References

Frantz, Fanon 1986 [1952].
Peau Noire, Masques Blancs 1952, *Black Skin, White Masks*. Charles Lan Markmann (transl.). New York: Grove Press 1967, reprint, 1986.

Fontaine, Marcel Djamala 1999.
A Visitor's Guide to Kwéyòl: An Intro to Reading & Writing of Antillean Kwéyòl. Roseau, Dominica: Paramount Printers Ltd.

Gadamer, Hans-Georg 1976 [1971].
Hegel's Dialectic: Five Hermeneutical Studies. New Haven and London: Yale University Press.

García Canclini, Néstor 1995.
Hybrid Cultures: Strategies for Entering and Leaving Modernity. C.L. Chippari and S.L. López (transl.). Minneapolis: University of Minnesota Press.

Gates, Henry Lewis Junior (ed.) 1987.
Classic Slave Narratives. New York: Penguin Books.

Gilroy, Paul 1992.
The Black Atlantic: Modernity and Double Consciousness. Cambridge: Harvard University Press.

Goodridge, Cecil A. 1972.
The French Connexion. In E. O. LeBlanc (ed), *Aspects of Dominican History*. Roseau, Dominica: Government Printing Division, pp. 157–162.

Government of Dominica, Central Statistics Office 1996.
Travel Report 1996. Roseau: Government Printers.

Gussler, Judith G. 1980.
Adaptive Strategies and Social Networks of Women in St. Kitts. In Erika Bourguignon (ed.), *World of Women. Anthropological Studies of Women in the Societies of the World*. New York: Praeger.

Hannerz, Ulf 1987.
The World in Creolisation. *Africa* 57: 546–559.

Hannerz, Ulf 1992.
Cultural Complexity. New York: Columbia University Press.

List of References

Hegel, G. W. F. 1807.
The Phenomenology of Mind.

Honychurch, Lennox 1995.
The Dominica Story. London and Basingstoke: MacMillan Education Limited.

Honychurch, Lennox 1994.
Folklore/Festivals. In *Dominica's Arts and Culture.*
A publication of the Cultural Division, Ministry of Community Development and Social Affairs, Commonwealth of Dominica, pp. 27–28.

Kalinago Barana Autê website
http://www.kalinagobaranaaute.com/. Accessed October 16, 2008.

Khan, Aisha 2001.
Journey to the Center of the Earth: The Caribbean as Master Symbol. *Cultural Anthropology* 16(3): 271–302.

Manuel, Peter 1995.
Caribbean Currents: Caribbean Music from Rumba to Reggae. Philadelphia: Temple University Press.

Maurer Bill 2000.
Sexualities and Separate Spheres: Gender, Sexual Identity, and Work in Dominica and Beyond. In *Gender Matters: Re-Reading Michelle Z. Rosaldo*, Lugo and Maurer (eds.). Ann Arbor: Univ. of Michigan Press, pp. 90–115.

Mintz, Sidney 1977.
The So-Called World System: Local Initiatives and Local Responses. *Dialectical Anthropology* 2(2): 253–270.

Mintz, Sidney and Richard Price 1992.
The Birth of African-American Culture: An Anthropological Perspective. Boston: Beacon Press.

Munasinghe, Viranjini. 2006.
Theorizing World Culture through the New World: East Indians and Creolization. *American Ethnologist* 33(4): 549–562.

Mourillon, V.J. Francis n.d.
The Dominica Banana Industry from Inception to Independence 1928–1978. Roseau, Dominica: Tropical Printers Ltd., W.I.

Myers, Gordon 2004.
Banana Wars, the Price of Free Trade. London and New York: Zed Books.

Nurse, Keith and Wayne Sandiford 1995.
Windward Islands Bananas – Challenges and Options under the Single European Market. Jamaica: Friedrich Ebert Stiftung.

Ott, P. J. 2003.
Dominica: Where Visitors Can be Part of the Wildlife. *Wild Side Destinations* CulturalTravels.com Volume 4, December 2002. Accessed August 3, 2003.

Papastergiadis, Nikos 1997.
Tracing Hybridity in Theory. In *Debating Cultural Hybridity: Multicultural Identities and the Politics of Anti-racism*, P. Werbner and T. Modood (eds.). London: Zed Books, pp. 257–281.

Patullo, Polly 2005.
Last Resorts: The Cost of Tourism in the Caribbean, 2nd edition. New York: New York University Press.

Patullo, Polly 2006.
Massive Exposure for Dominica in Latest "Pirates of the Caribbean" Movie. *The Guardian.* July 12, 2006.

Phillip, Daryl and Gary Smith 1998.
The Heritage Dances of Dominica. Heritage Awareness Programme, Dominica Division of Culture Community Development. Roseau, Dominica: Government of Dominica.

Price, Richard 2007.
Some Anthropological Musings on Creolization. *Journal of Pidgin and Creole Languages* 22(1): 17–36.

Proesmans, Fr. R. 1972.
Notes on the Slaves of the French. In *Aspects of Dominican History*, E. O. LeBlanc (ed.). Roseau, Dominica: Government Printing Division, pp.163–172.

Quinlan, Marsha B. 2004.
> *From the Bush: The Front Line of Health Care in a Caribbean Village.* Belmont, CA: Wadsworth Press.

Rosaldo, Renato 1989.
> Imperialist Nostalgia. *Representations* No. 26, Special Issue: Memory and Counter-Memory (Spring, 1989), pp. 107–122.

Rose, Deidre 2009.
> Telling Treasure Tales: Commemoration and Consciousness in Dominica. *Journal of American Folklore.*

Rose, Deidre 2005.
> *Morality Plays: Popular Theatre for AIDS Awareness in the Commonwealth of Dominica, WI.* Doctoral Dissertation, University of Toronto.

Scobie, Edward 1965.
> *Dies Dominica. A Publication Commemorating Dominica Day.* Dominica.

Sheller, Mimi 2003.
> *Consuming the Caribbean: From Arawaks to Zombies.* London and New York: Routledge.

Sheller, Mimi 2007.
> Virtual Islands: Mobilities, Connectivity, and the New Caribbean Spatialities. *Small axe* 24: 16–33

Sloat, Susanna (ed.) 2005.
> *Caribbean Dance from Abakua to Zouk: How Movement Shapes Identity.* Florida: University Press of Florida.

Slocum, Karla and Deborah A. Thomas 2003.
> Rethinking Global and Area Studies: Insights from Caribbeanist Anthropology. *American Anthropologist* 105(3): 553–565.

Smith, Kelvin 2006
> Placing the Carib Model Village: The Carib Territory and Dominican Tourism.In *Indigenous resurgence in the Contemporary Caribbean – Amerindian Survival and Revival,.* Maximillian Forte (ed.). New York: Peter Lang Publishing Inc, pp. 71–87.

Sobo, Elisa J 1993.

One Blood: The Jamaican Body. New York: SUNY Press.

Stewart, Charles (ed.) 2007.

Creolization: History, Ethnography, Theory. Walnut Creek, CA: Left Coast Press Inc.

Stewart, Charles 1999.

Syncretism and its Synonyms: Reflections on Cultural Mixture. *Diacritics* 29(3): 40–62.

Stoler, Ann and Frederick Cooper 1997.

Between Metropole and Colony. Rethinking a Research Agenda. In *The Tensions of Empire,* Frederick Cooper and Ann Laura Stoler (eds.). Berkeley: University of California Press, pp.1–56.

Trouillot, Michel-Rolph 2002.

Culture on the Edges: Caribbean Creolization in Historical Context. In *From the Margins: Historical Anthropology and its Futures*, Brian Keith Axel (ed.). Durham, NC: Duke University Press, pp. 189–210.
1988. *Peasants and Capital: Dominica in the World Economy.* Baltimore: Johns Hopkins University Press.
1992. The Caribbean Region: An Open Frontier in Anthropological Theory. *Annual Review of Anthropology* 21: 19–42.
1993. Coffee Planters and Coffee Slaves: From Saint Dominigue to Dominica. In *Cultivation and Culture: The Shaping of Slave Life in the Americas*, I. Berlin & P Morgan (eds.). Charlottesville, VA: University of Virginia Press.

Tylor, Edward B. 1871

Primitive Culture, Volume 1: *The Origins of Culture.* York: Harper and Row.

Werbner, Pnina 1997.

Introduction: The Dialectics of Cultural Hybridity. In *Debating cultural hybridity: multi-cultural identities and the politics of anti-racism*, P. Werbner and T. Modood (eds.). London: Zed Books, pp. 1–26.

Werbner, Pnina, and Tariq Modood (eds.) 1997.

Debating Cultural Hybridity: Multi-Cultural Identities and the Politics of Anti-Racism. London: Zed Books.

List of References

Williams, Chief Charles 2005.

> Statement from Chief Charles Williams of the Dominica Carib Territory. http://openanthropology.wordpress.com/2005/02/18/ statement-from-chief-charles-williams-of-the-dominica-carib-territory-re-disney/. Accessed October 18, 2008.

Wilson, Peter 1973.

> *Crab Antics: A Caribbean Study of the Conflict Between Reputation and Respectability.* New Haven: Yale University Press.

Wissing, Douglas 1999.

> "Dominica: Call of the Wild" Special to *The Washington Post* Sunday, February 28, 1999; Page E01. http://www.washingtonpost.com/wp-srv/travel/destinations/caribbean/dominica022899.htm. Accessed August 3, 2003.

Young, Robert J. C. 1994.

> *Colonial Desire: Hybridity in Theory, Culture and Race.* New York and London: Routledge.

Whitfield, Harvey Amani 2005.

> *From American Slaves to Nova Scotian Subjects: The Case of the Black Refugees, 1813–1840.* Toronto: Pearson, Prentice Hall.

World Creole Music Festival, official web-site.

> http://www.wcmfdominica.com/aboutthefestival.php. Accessed October 19, 2008.